Lillian's Flying School

a novel
by Nancy Lammers

THE BRIDGE

The Bridge
Huntersville, NC

Cover art: Nancy Lammers
Photo of cover art: Ken Pedersen
Cover design: Ann Campanella
Author photo: Judy Freeman

Lillian's Flying School is a work of fiction. Names, characters, places and incidents are either made up from the author's imagination or have been used fictitiously. Any similarity to actual events, places or persons, living or dead, is entirely coincidental.

ISBN-13: 978-0692129654
ISBN-10: 0692129650

Produced in the United States of America

The Bridge
Huntersville, NC
www.thebridgebooks.com

For anyone who has ever wanted to fly

and my sister,
Myra

Contents

Introduction

Lillian Brown, a middle-aged family counselor and single parent is almost overwhelmed attempting to meet the expectations of her adult daughter and the increasing demands of her job. After an unusually chaotic day, she dreams she can fly. When her dream becomes a reality and she begins giving flying lessons to a troubled sixteen-year-old boy, a couple living in a retirement community, and a married woman and her six-year-old daughter, unexpected and unsettling events occur in all their lives.

Not only are her life and the lives of her students' families affected, but the lives of the entire small town of Green Valley as well.

Lillian's Flying School is a parable about the bonds of friendship, family and community, and the transforming power of love.

Chapter 1
Lillian Has a Long Day

Lillian Brown stepped out of the elevator onto the silent, shadowy fifth floor of the Green Valley Human Resources building. She hurried down the hall toward the Family Counseling Offices, carrying an armful of magazines that she'd collected from her neighbors. The magazines were for clients to look at while they waited for their appointments.

She had unzipped her green quilted parka and unwound the red and white striped scarf from around her neck. The scarf hung over her shoulders, the fringed ends flapping against her knees as she walked. A few strands of wavy, red hair stuck out from her red and white knit cap and drooped across her forehead. She huffed a couple of breaths at her hair and sighed. What was she going to do about Karen? The phone conversation she'd had earlier with her daughter played in her mind like a looped recording.

And her job? How could she be such an experienced counselor and have let her own life get so out of control?

She paused and drew in a long breath. If only she could throw out her arms, leap into the air and fly away. But of course, she wouldn't even if she could. Unthinkable.

She yanked off her knit cap and stuffed it in her shoulder bag on top of her red knit gloves. Here she'd had to come in thirty minutes early just to fill out those agency evaluation forms that had to be turned in by the end of the day because the rest of her day was already full. Back-to-back appointments. That speech at the board of directors' meeting at noon.

"I'm sorry," Dr. Will Hawkins, her supervisor had said, striding into her office just as she was leaving work the day before. He'd plunked down the evaluation forms on her desk. "I really appreciate your doing these forms. I hate I've had to be away so much the past month or so." His eyes had narrowed as he looked at her. "Things will slow down before too much longer."

Lillian wasn't so sure. Ever since he published his book, *Absent Parenting*, three months ago, he'd been so busy giving talks and TV interviews he'd not had time to do many of the requirements of his own job.

At first, she'd been glad to help out, but lately he'd started asking her also to supervise the office when he was away and notify him of problems. After the third or fourth time, she finally said, "Will, I can continue doing this, but I'd like some kind of a promotion with enough authority to handle the usual kinds of things. Otherwise I'd rather not do it anymore. The way it is now, I'm like a kid writing the names of misbehaving students on the blackboard when the teacher's out of the room."

Will had shaken his head, said simply that there was no provision for a promotion in the budget, and that he would still count on her since she was the senior counselor.

Stuck. That's what she was. Here she was, fifty years old, divorced, and living alone. The way she saw it her only option was to look for another job. But, these days counseling positions were almost non-existent.

Besides, where else could she find a job with a better-than-average steady paycheck and great benefits? In addition, she'd been with the agency seventeen years. She liked her clients and her coworkers, even Will Hawkins. When he was in the office. Not off somewhere signing books.

Lillian stopped in front of the door to the suite of counseling offices and fished in her handbag for her keys.

Once inside, she flipped on the overhead lights in the reception area. Sputtering light flickered on the closed doors of the six offices lined up side by side on the adjacent outside walls. In front of her a red light blinked on the secretary's desk phone. Lillian sighed. These days everyone had problems.

She walked in front of the secretary's desk and spread out her armful of magazines on the table beside the green, vinyl sofa that was against the inside wall.

Next, she walked back across the reception area and into her office, the one closest to the door. She switched on the overhead light and glanced at the neat stack of evaluation forms on her desk. The scarred oak desk sat against the wall next to the single floor-to-ceiling window. The blinds over the window were closed.

A chipped black-enameled coat rack that Lillian had bought at a yard sale stood in a corner of the room next to an unpainted wood bookcase. The bookcase held five shelves of books about different kinds of counseling techniques which Lillian rarely looked at anymore. Her framed counselor's diploma hung on the wall above the bookcase.

Draping her parka, scarf, and cap on the coat rack, she walked between three metal folding chairs to the window. She twisted the clear, plastic rod hanging at one side of the blinds. The blinds remained closed. She twisted the rod again. Nothing.

"Never fails!" she muttered, kicking off her shoes. Holding onto the arms of her desk chair, she centered one knee on the seat, then slowly crawled onto her desk.

She stood and inched her way to the edge of the desk closest to the window. Rising onto her tiptoes, she reached up under the metal top of the blinds where it was attached to the window frame. She slipped her finger around the cord and pulled. "Come on, come on," she whispered. "We need some light in here."

"Good grief!" boomed Will Hawkins' voice from behind her. "What on earth are you doing up there?"

Lillian jumped. "Heeeelp!" she shrieked, lurching forward, her hands and arms plunging through the slats of the blinds. Barely yanking her arms free, she stumbled back onto her desk as the blinds ripped from the wall and crashed to the floor.

Will Hawkins rushed toward her. "Watch out! Watch out!" His face was red above his short clipped, black beard. His navy and white striped silk tie swung haphazardly across the lapels of his dark blue jacket. But with his gaze on Lillian instead of the floor, his trim, fit, six-foot-three-inch body tripped over the waste basket, and he crashed into her desk.

The desk slammed against the wall, throwing Lillian off balance again as wadded-up papers, pencil shavings, dried-up tea bags and a lone piece of orange peel flew out of the waste basket and scattered across the mottled beige floor tiles.

Waving her arms, Lillian danced about on the top of her desk, trying to regain her balance and at the same time not trip over her computer and Will Hawkins who was now sprawled across the desk at her feet.

At last steady, she gawked down at him. Poor dignified, proper Dr. Will. Always so in control. She suppressed a giggle. Behind her, January morning sunlight spilled through the tall, bare window into her office. At least it wasn't dark and dreary anymore. But so what about that?

Will Hawkins slowly pushed himself upright, lifted his hands from the desk, and stepped back. He staggered a little. Lillian scooted down off her desk and onto the floor. "Will, are you all right? Easy, easy. Take a deep breath."

Will Hawkins flung out his arms. "I don't need a breath," he gasped. "I'm perfectly fine." Glaring, his eyes wide and dark, he straightened his tie and pulled down his jacket sleeves.

"If there was a problem with the blinds, you should've called maintenance. You could have fallen and gotten hurt. Seriously hurt."

Lillian shook her head and grinned. "Not me. I'd have just spread out my arms and flown."

Will stared at her. "That is not funny. That is not funny at all." He frowned. Then he picked his way through the papers and trash to the doorway. He turned and looked back at her. His shoulders drooped slightly. He spoke softly as if to a child that was unable to fully grasp the situation. "You have always been my most responsible counselor. I've always known what to expect from you. At least you were on time today. As usual."

"Thanks." Was being on time that surprising? "Thanks," she said again, raising her voice, but he'd already turned and was walking out of her office and across the reception room with his head down. He disappeared into his office.

From out in the hall came the sounds of Sherry, their secretary, and the four other family counselors talking and laughing on their way in. Lillian closed her door and glanced at the big metal rimmed clock over her door. 8:25. Too late now to do those evaluation forms.

After gathering up the papers that had been scattered across the floor and dumping the rest of the trash back in the waste basket, Lillian shoved the blinds back against the wall. She looked up just as a flock of tiny brown sparrows flew past her window. She watched until they were out of sight. Wonderful little creatures.

She closed her eyes and pictured herself balanced on the window ledge, flying off into an air current, soaring high as a cloud, swooping back and forth above the buildings. She breathed deeply. She could almost feel the wind against her cheeks.

She opened her eyes. She actually felt a lifting inside her. Then she looked at her phone and sighed. Plus, all the appointments and speech, there were two notes. "Make cake for office party" and "Karen's cats." She thought back to that distressing phone call with her daughter earlier. Karen had gotten so upset she'd hung up before Lillian could even finish her sentence.

Her cell phone dinged, and a message popped up on its screen: "Your first clients are here." Lillian placed the phone, face down on her desk, took a long breath, held it to the count of eight and exhaled slowly.

She opened the door and smiled at a pale, thin young woman and her scowling eight-year-old son. "Hello," she said brightly. "Come on in. I'm glad to see you."

The young woman nodded and walked inside. She stared at the bare window and the blinds, lying in a heap on the floor. She adjusted the strap of her over-the-shoulder bag. The boy walked over and kicked the blinds with the toe of his sneaker. The shoe laces in both sneakers were untied. The ends of the laces flopped about in what seemed to Lillian a defiant sort of way. He glared at Lillian through a mop of shaggy brown hair and kicked the blinds again. "How come they're down there?"

"Umm. Well." Lillian straightened her shoulders and spoke in her calm, firm, no-apologies-needed voice. "I pulled them down. By accident of course." She smiled at the boy's mother and shrugged in what she intended as a shared woundedness kind of way. She motioned toward the chairs. "Would you like to have a seat, so we can get started?"

Chapter 2
Lillian Has a Dream

It was late when Lillian drove into the parking lot of her apartment building complex. Lights glowed from the lamp posts in the parking lot and in most of the apartment windows. On the ground floor, only her apartment was dark.

Usually she parked right in front. Tonight, a car was already in that place. She had to park at the end on the opposite side of the lot. But at least she'd finally completed those evaluation papers, and all her files were up to date. Her speech at the board of directors' noon meeting also had gone well. At least a few of the members had seemed sympathetic to her plea not to cut staff positions and had said they'd think about what she'd said.

After eating a bowl of soup and a sandwich, Lillian pulled out her mixer, bowl and measuring cups and set them on the kitchen counter. She was in the middle of making the cake for the office party when her cell phone rang.

"Hello, Mom?"

"Karen! How are you? Wait, hang on." Lillian turned off the mixer, touched the speaker button on her phone, and laid the phone on the counter. "How'd your interview go?" She scraped batter off the beaters and into the bowl. She pictured Karen, sitting cross-legged in the middle of a motel room bed, her long auburn hair pulled behind her ears. In the background she heard TV voices.

"Not so good. The company said they liked it that I had a college degree but they wanted someone with a business major instead of economics. They said they needed someone with more experience than working one year as cashier in a gift shop."

Lillian listened to Karen breathe in and out a couple of times. When Karen spoke again her voice was hesitant.

"Mom, about this morning. I'm sorry I got mad at you for suggesting I ask my neighbors to turn down their stereo. It wasn't you. You know how much stress I've been under." She paused. "Anyway, I heard about an opening in another company in this same town. They can talk to me tomorrow and ...."

"And would I mind taking care of your cats another day or two, so you can stay over?" Usually Lillian didn't mind because her apartments didn't allow pets. It was actually relaxing to play with the cats for a few minutes. But Karen lived all the way

18

across town, and tonight Lillian had been late leaving the office. Besides checking on the cats, she'd also had to go to the store to get the cake mix for the office party. She hadn't had a free moment all day. And the rest of the week was about the same.

"Mo-om, I thought you liked them."

"Honey, I do. Really. I love your cats. It's just that...." She sighed. "All right. I'll be glad to. To take care of them." In a way she did want to because she wanted Karen to be as relaxed as possible for her interview. She wanted Karen to find a job she would be happy with almost as much as Karen did.

Truthfully, it was hard for Lillian to say "no" to Karen about anything. Ever since Karen's father walked out on them, seventeen years ago, when Karen was only seven, it had just been the two of them. Even though she knew better she still kept trying to make it up to Karen for having to grow up in a single parent home.

After ending the call, Lillian finished the cake and cleaned up the kitchen. She hoped Karen's interview went well. With both Karen and Will Hawkins leaning on her, she was starting to feel confined and burned out.

She pictured the sparrows that had flown past her office window that morning. So beautiful and free. What wouldn't she give, right now, to fly away and leave it all behind?

That night when Lillian climbed into bed, she lay awake for a long time with thoughts about her day roiling inside her head like a storm at sea. When she finally fell asleep, she dreamed that she was standing in the middle of a wide open meadow, bordered by tall trees. Then as if she'd known all along that she could, she jumped, spread out her arms, and flew into the sky.

She woke up with her heart beating so fast she could hardly breathe. It had been so vivid, so real she almost couldn't believe it was only a dream. But of course it was, for here she was in her own bed. Even so. Didn't dreams often precede reality? How much difference was there, really, between a dream and its reality? She snuggled under the blankets and squeezed her eyes shut.

A memory popped into her mind. She was a child of six, standing on the edge of her grandparents' back porch. Her grandfather stood on the ground beneath her with his arms stretched toward her.

"I'm going to jump," she yelled.

"I'll catch you," her grandfather called back.

Then she jumped as high as she could. Her red hair had frizzed out from her head as her toes left the porch. She had looked up between her fingers. Nothing but sky. Then, right at the height of the jump, just before falling, there'd been a moment of weightlessness. It was scarcely more than a slight hesitation. But she still remembered, in that moment, a kind of glorious knowing that all things were possible. If only she could figure out how to stretch that moment of weightlessness, she was sure she could fly.

Chapter 3
Lillian Extends Weightlessness

The next morning, as soon as the alarm went off, Lillian sat up and swung her legs over the edge of her bed. She stood with both feet on the small multi-colored braided rug beside her bed. But before stepping into her fuzzy pink slippers, she crouched halfway to the floor and jumped as high as she could. Got to start practicing. Got to start stretching that moment of weightlessness.

At work, between clients, she started closing her door. Sometimes she practiced jumping. Other times she just sat at her desk, closed her eyes and imagined herself inside that tiny moment of weightlessness at the height of the jumps. Each time she strained to stretch that moment longer than the time before.

One day, several weeks later, while she was imagining, she felt a slight tingling in the soles of her feet. The next day when she stepped off the curb at an

21

intersection, there was a slight hesitation before her foot touched down onto the street. Shivers ran up and down her spine. It was happening. She just knew it. Soon she was going to fly.

During the following days and weeks, Lillian went nowhere except to work and to a zoning meeting at the town hall. She turned down two dinner invitations from Sylvia and Ed Jeffers, her oldest and closest friends. They lived down the block from where she used to live when she was married. They had been almost like family.

When Karen called to say that both of the companies who'd interviewed her had hired other people, Lillian had been so busy jumping and concentrating on weightlessness, she scarcely worried. After all, wasn't Karen an adult and plenty savvy? Lillian was sure that sooner or later she'd find the right job. And sooner or later, Lillian had to stop imagining she could fly and actually try to do it.

Day by day she put off trying. She made excuses. There wasn't enough time. She had other more pressing work to do. She was too tired after a long day of work. But the real reason was that she was afraid she'd only discover that it was hopeless, and she would never fly, that it had all been an impossible dream.

Finally, one evening the urge to fly was so strong she couldn't resist it any longer. She couldn't even sit still long enough to listen to the evening news after dinner.

Walking into her living room, she kicked off her shoes. She shoved the coffee table back against the sofa and pushed the dining table and chairs against the wall, next to her old upright piano. She stood in the middle of the room and looked at the space she had created around her. Was this enough room? How much would she actually need?

She looked at the two large butterfly pictures hanging over the sofa and at the gold and orange maple leaf painting above her lavender-flowered easy chair by the door.

Lillian had painted the butterfly pictures and Sylvia had painted the leaf painting. One winter, they had taken art lessons at the community center. Sylvia had given her painting to Lillian at the time of her divorce. The painting was of the maple tree behind Lillian's former house.

Lillian looked closely at the painting. Did she see movement in the leaves? Sense their buoyancy? Tingling started in the soles of her feet again. The feeling grew stronger. It flowed up her legs and out her arms to the tips of her fingers, up her body to her neck and on up to the top of her head.

Drawing in a breath so full her lungs pushed out her ribs, she stooped almost to the floor. Exhaling, she threw her arms over her head and jumped. But her toes only rose level with the top of the coffee table before she dropped.

Maybe she needed height. Climbing onto the arm of the sofa, she jumped again. She sailed over the coffee table like a flying fish, but then she landed on the floor in a heap.

She sat up and rubbed her elbow where it had scraped on the carpet. At least she wasn't bleeding, and nothing seemed broken. She smacked her face. Of course. She hadn't imagined weightlessness. And what if she started off a little higher? Then she'd have more time to imagine.

But first she gathered up all the sofa pillows. She arranged them side by side on top of the coffee table and on the floor in front of it. Just in case. She was a little battered and bruised from her falls.

"Weightlessness, weightlessness," she whispered over and over as she climbed onto the back of the sofa. She stood up and leaned against the wall a moment to steady herself. The top of her head was only a few inches from the ceiling.

Holding out her arms for balance, she closed her eyes. She imagined her bones being hollow, her entire body light as a moth's.

Taking a full breath, she jumped, thrusting her arms out in front of her. She hung suspended for a moment as if resting on a column of air. But then she crashed. At least that was the idea. She sat up in the middle of the pillows and hugged herself.

What was she missing? Could it be something obvious? *Bicycle riding.* The words surfaced in her mind like water bubbling up from a mountain spring.

She climbed back onto the top of the sofa and stood. Picturing herself light as air, she jumped. At the same time, she threw her arms straight out in front and drew her feet and legs up into a line with her body. "Move forward," she said to herself. "Keep moving forward. The way you balance riding a bicycle."

She hovered over the coffee table and all the piled-up pillows. But then she glided forward, only an inch or so below the ceiling. Beneath her, the paintings on the walls, the upright piano and dining table and chairs slid past. As if she had been doing this all her life, she flew all the way across the living room.

Just before crashing into the wall above the front door, she lowered her arms and ducked her head. She tumbled onto the seat of her lavender-flowered easy chair. Tears filled her eyes. "I did it," she whispered, drawing up her knees to her chin and circling her arms around her legs. "I, Lillian Brown, have finally taught myself to fly."

After flying off the back of the sofa several times, Lillian decided to try simply jumping off the floor. Not a problem. She shook her head and hugged herself again. Height wasn't necessary at all. It was simply figuring out all the right steps. Soon she was flying around the living room as naturally as if she had been born with wings.

Being careful not to bump her head on the top of the door jamb, she flew from the living room into her tiny kitchen, then down the short hall to her bedroom. Just for fun, she flew around and around her apartment until it was time for bed. She was so excited she could hardly sleep. What would Will Hawkins and her coworkers say if she told them how she'd spent her evening? So funny! She laughed out loud just imagining the expressions on their faces.

Chapter 4

Lillian Flies Above the Meadow

The next morning as she drove to work, Lillian decided to wait before telling anyone about having learned to fly. It was still too new. She needed to get used to it herself first.

But by the weekend, she felt confined only flying around her apartment. She wanted to fly higher. Farther.

She looked at the calendar on her phone. Tomorrow was Saturday. Nothing typed on it. Usually Karen came over and they went to the mall. But Karen had said this time she needed to work on her resume and planned to go to a career workshop. She really should call Sylvia and Ed. It had been weeks since she'd promised to get in a visit with them. She closed the calendar and put down her phone. One more day wouldn't matter. How long had it been since she had had an entire free day?

Early the next morning, as soon as Lillian finished breakfast, she pulled on jeans and a heavy sweater, packed a bag lunch and filled a thermos with coffee. Then she wrapped her long red and white knit scarf around her neck, pulled the matching cap down over her ears and dashed outside to her car. After scraping off the windshield, she slid behind the steering wheel.

In minutes, she was singing made-up words to a made-up country-style tune while she drove down the interstate, heading for the country. She tapped the steering wheel with her little finger as she sang, "I've been flying, room to room; flying in my little home; now I want to fly outside; want to fly into the sky; see how far that I can go." She sang the same words over and over.

Just before the Green Valley city limits sign, a woods appeared on her side. Lillian glanced out the car window through the bare branches of the trees and gasped. In the center was a meadow. Just like the one in her dream.

She turned off at the next exit and drove down a twisting, graveled road that dead-ended at the edge of the meadow. After parking by a fallen tree, she locked her car, put the key in her shoe then waded through tall brown grass to the middle of the meadow.

She looked beyond the grasses to the trees, their bare branches like large, brown, lacy fans against the sky. Above the trees, the sky was blue with shreds of white clouds. The air was still and cold, filled with the musty odors of dried leaves and cold damp earth. Her

28

breath came in small white puffs. Not a sound, not even a bird call.

Now. The word coursed through her. *Now.* Taking a full deep breath, she rose onto her toes and stretched her arms over her head. Dropping her arms, she stooped and jumped.

Up, up, up. Air whizzed past her arms, body and legs that were stretched straight into a slender line. The ends of her red and white scarf flapped at her side. Wisps of reddish hair sticking out of her cap blew flat against her cheeks and forehead while the trees dropped below in a blur. She flew higher and higher until, far below, the meadow shrunk tiny as the scenery on a toy train display.

Wonderful! Wonderful! The words sang inside her. She kicked her legs like she was swimming in air, waved large circles with her arms, dipped and spun her body like a dancer. How could she possibly be doing what she was doing?

She dove into an air current and spiraled upward into the middle of a cold misty cloud. Cupping her fingers, the moist air pushed against the palms of her hands. Cold water droplets stung her face as she flew on through the cloud into blue sky. Tears blurred her eyes. *Wonderful! Simply wonderful!*

She angled into a down draft and hurtled toward the ground like she was on a roller coaster. The force of the air almost pulled off her stocking cap and flattened her red and white knit scarf against her side. Almost touching the top branches of the trees, she raised her arms until her body leveled. She swooped back and forth over the trees several times then flew back into the sky. She zigzagged high above the meadow the rest of the morning.

Finally, deciding it must be almost noon because she was so hungry, she circled the meadow one last time and landed on her feet. Her legs wobbled when she tried to walk. The ground rose and fell. Staggering, she tossed the ends of her scarf over her shoulders and laughed.

Whoever would have believed anything so wonderful was possible? She, ordinary Lillian Brown, had learned to fly.

After taking her lunch bag and insulated coffee container from the car, she sat on a log at the edge of the meadow. She took out her sandwich and opened the lid on her coffee container. While she sipped coffee, she stared through the tops of the bare trees. It was too wonderful. She couldn't keep flying a secret any longer.

She'd tell Karen first. And offer to teach her.

Lillian smiled. She leaned back and looked up at the cloud she'd just flown through. Maybe even teach a few others. Yes. She'd love to do that. Have her own flying school.

As soon as she returned home, she phoned Karen, but her daughter didn't pick up. She left a message and tried again later. She tried again on Sunday afternoon and evening. Was she still at the workshop? Wherever she was, she hoped the workshop was helpful and that

30

Karen was having a good time. Lillian decided not to wait any longer.

On Monday morning before her first client arrived, she called the Green Valley Times. "I want to place a classified ad," she said to the receptionist, "to read: 'Flying lessons. Experienced instructor. Guaranteed to teach you how to fly. Call (and she listed her cell phone number) after 6:00 p.m. for additional information.'"

Chapter 5
The Classified Ad

Lillian's ad appeared in the newspaper the next day. After work, as soon as she slipped behind the wheel of her car, she checked her phone for messages, Only three numbers with no identification. But it was only 5:30 and she'd put "after 6:00" in her ad. Even so, someone could have been too eager to wait.

Then, just as she walked up the icy steps from the parking lot in front of her apartment, the silvery harp chords on her phone sounded. Swiping the phone and pressing it to her ear, she said, "Hello." Hurrying, she shoved the key in the lock of her apartment door and raced inside. "Hello?" She dashed into the hall, and grabbed a spiral notebook that was lying on her desk. "FLYING SCHOOL STUDENTS; 8:00 a.m. Saturday Mornings" was printed on the top line.

"Ms. L. Brown?" said a man.

"Yes. Speaking."

"This is Carlton with ACME Development Company. We are proud to notify you that you have just won a free weekend at our beach resort. All you have to do is tour our new luxury beach front condominiums, and—"

"Whoa. Sorry, but I'm not interested." As soon as she put down the phone it rang again.

"Mom, it's me, Karen. Good news."

"Wonderful." Lillian smiled. "I've got some too. I tried to call you. I left a message I—"

"Mom. You didn't let me finish. I didn't get back until late. I went to that career planning workshop this weekend like I said. A representative from Bryant Securities was one of the presenters. I went out to eat with a couple of their employees afterwards. And I've got an interview with one of them. Next Monday. The guy leading the workshop said I should apply for a position. As a stock broker. He said I'd be good at it. But Bryant's is an old company and they really dress well. Will you go shopping with me Saturday and help me pick out something to wear to the interview?"

Lillian held her breath a moment. "I'm so happy for you, That's wonderful news about the interview." She looked through the kitchen window into the night sky. Light from the parking lot lamp posts sent out a pale yellowish glow. Across the lot a car was pulling into a parking space. "Honey, I hate to do the least thing to disappoint you, but I can't go shopping this Saturday. I'm—I'm probably going to be busy."

"Doing what?"

"That's what I was trying to call you about. I'm—um—starting a flying school. I'd love for you to come too, so I can show you. Maybe we can go shopping afterwards. See, I've learned how to fly and…."

"Mother, what are you talking about?"

"Honey, I just told you. I learned how to fly, and now I'm going to give flying lessons. I wanted to tell you first, but I never could reach you. I was so excited. I couldn't wait any longer. I'm running an ad in the paper and…."

"Mother! Be serious! This just happens to be the most important interview in my whole life." And before Lillian could even say, "Good luck" and "You don't really need me to help you choose something to wear," Karen hung up.

As soon as Lillian put down her phone, it rang again.

"Uh, hello," a male voice said. "What's this about flying lessons? Which airport? And what kind of planes?"

Lillian wiped her hands on her denim skirt and swallowed. "We're not using planes. I'm going to teach you how to jump into the air, spread out your arms, and…."

"Lady, what are you? Some kind of nut?" The phone went silent.

The next call was from a young married woman, Marty Jones, who worked out of her home doing the book keeping for the family landscaping business. She said she got lonely not seeing anyone and thought taking a class would be a good way to meet people. "You're sure this isn't a joke?"

Lillian explained that she'd give a demonstration first to prove it was possible. She added that the demonstration would be free, and that since this was her first time teaching flying, fees would be whatever each student wanted to pay. Later on, if this class was successful, then she would charge a regular fee.

"I never dreamed of such a thing," Marty said. "When I tell my husband, Harry, that at 8:00 a.m., Saturday morning, I'm going to watch a woman jump into the air and fly, he'll say I'm wasting my time even to watch, much less try it myself."

Lillian sighed. "He wouldn't be the first."

"What? Well, I'm coming. Where should I go?"

"There's a meadow just north of downtown. Take the gravel road after the first exit and go all the way to the end. I'll tack a sign, LILLIAN'S FLYING SCHOOL, to a tree."

After Lillian had eaten dinner and watched the news, she sat down at her piano and played the made-up melody to her made-up song about flying. She sang the same words over and over as she improvised variations.

The phone rang. This time it was a teenaged boy, Robby Fulton. "We won't be *on* anything? This I got to try."

Lillian sighed as she wrote his name under Marty Jones in the spiral notebook. "Oh, and you'll need to bring your parents' written permission with you."

After Robby, no one else called. Before going to bed, Lillian flew around her apartment several times to reassure herself that she really could fly. All the doubts she'd been hearing were making her feel a little unsure.

Chapter 6

The Town Hall Meeting

The next evening Lillian attended a meeting at town hall. The issue to be discussed was another involving zoning. A woman had complained about her next-door neighbor's two pet goats breaking out of their pen and eating up her daylilies. Lillian was especially interested in this because when Karen was a child, she had had a pet goat along with three gerbils, a cat and a dog. Back then there hadn't even been leash laws. No question but that the town was growing. And changing.

In the reception area Lillian ran into her friends, Sylvia and Ed Jeffers. They had unzipped their jackets and loosened their scarves and were talking Theodore Green, a town councilman, and his wife, Agnes. The Greens, along with Sylvia and Ed, had been former neighbors of Lillian's.

Theodore was fingering the collar of his tweed sports jacket in an agitated manner as if he wanted to go on inside even though it was still fifteen minutes before the meeting was scheduled to start. Both of the Greens were tall and thin, the expressions on their faces perpetually tense and serious.

Lillian's relationship with them had never been close, but it had grown increasingly distant in recent years. Usually, now, whenever she ran into them in a store or on the street, they informed her of some misdeed that her ex-husband had committed since he was still living in the same house across the street from the Greens. He had not rolled back the recycle bin from the street curb in a timely fashion. He was neglecting to cut off the dead branches on the trees in his yard. There were tall, unsightly weeds growing in his lawn.

Each time Lillian replied as nicely as she could that whatever her ex did was not her responsibility. But they never seemed to hear her.

Tonight Theodore and Agnes merely glanced in her direction and continued their conversation with Sylvia and Ed.

"Hello," Lillian said, smiling at the four of them. "Hello," she said again, louder.

Theodore drew in his cheeks and looked straight in her eyes. "There have been complaints about your husband's compost container—that it attracts dogs."

Lillian shook her head. "Please don't tell me. I hardly ever see him. I—"

"Might be a good idea if you did," Theodore said and nodded at Agnes who nodded back at him. Gripping Agnes's elbow, he looked at Sylvia and Ed, mumbled that he would be seeing them another time and steered Agnes toward the open doorway of the meeting hall.

"Where have you been hiding yourself?" Ed peered at Lillian through his wire-rimmed glasses. "We never see you anymore." He was wearing a beige, cable-knit pullover sweater under his jacket and dark brown corduroy slacks and loafers. He glanced at Sylvia who was still looking at Theodore and Agnes as they mingled with the people who were walking into the meeting room.

"I know," Sylvia said, turning back toward Lillian. Her eyes widened and a small wrinkle formed in the center of her forehead. She touched a thin gold chain that circled the neck of her pink turtleneck sweater. She combed her fingers through her curly blonde hair. "We haven't seen you for ages."

"I'm sorry," Lillian said. "I should have called long before now. I've been real busy. I mean...." She looked beyond Sylvia through the doorway into the meeting room. The last of the people in the reception area were now walking inside and settling into seats. "We'd better go on inside," she said. "I'll try to explain once we're seated."

She hated it that she hadn't contacted Sylvia before now. How could she have gotten so absorbed with flying that she'd forgotten her best friend? She'd been Sylvia's staunchest supporter when she opened her daycare center in that house beside the town green. She'd even spoken on Sylvia's behalf before the town zoning board.

Inside the meeting room, Lillian scanned the room. Only a few widely scattered empty seats remained. "I'm sorry, I guess we can't sit together. But I do want to catch you both up on things. We'll get together soon. Promise."

Sylvia half smiled. "Give us a call."

Lillian sighed and headed toward a chair near the back of the room. In a way, she was glad not to have to try to explain right then. She needed time to think about what exactly to say. She wasn't the same person she'd been seventeen years ago at the time of her separation. Her life was different now than it had been in those early years back when she and Sylvia had worked together on all those community committees and volunteer activities. Now flying mattered more than anything else. How could she best help Sylvia to understand?

When Lillian returned home, it was 10:15 and time for bed. She checked the messages on her phone. The only one was from George and Grace Wilson, a couple she'd met at a poetry writing workshop at the local bookstore. They had been high school sweethearts, having met at a swim meet when they were on opposing teams.

Grace was a retired physical therapist, and George had retired as principal of one of the local high schools. They lived in a condominium in a retirement community. When Lillian explained flying, would they still want to come? But she'd have to wait until tomorrow to find out. It was too late to call now.

Chapter 7
Lillian Meets Karen for Lunch

On Friday morning at work, after her first client had left, Lillian walked to the window. She stared down at the street at cars passing, people walking briskly, scarves and coat hems flapping. She gazed above the tops of buildings into the cloudy winter sky. Today was Friday. Tomorrow she would meet her flying students for the first time.

She had returned the Wilsons's call the night before. After reassuring them that age was not a factor, and she was sure their doctors would approve, they asked that their names be added to her list of students. Lillian tingled all over, thinking about her new venture.

But she still wanted to discuss it with Karen before her daughter heard the details from someone else. She glanced at her watch. Her second client was late. She picked up her cell phone and dialed the gift shop where Karen worked as cashier.

Maybe Karen could meet her for a quick lunch. They could discuss flying, plus visit. She hadn't talked to Karen since telling her she couldn't go shopping with her.

She certainly wasn't the obliging mother she'd been. Was she becoming too self-centered? Maybe, but she wasn't about to give up flying to be otherwise. She shrugged. If she had been her own client, she knew she would have urged her client-self to go for it. She sighed. It was hard to change old patterns of behavior.

At noon, when Lillian walked into LITTLE CHICK'S, warm moist air from frying chicken and fish enveloped her. Above the sounds of people talking and laughing, metal handles banged as wire baskets of sizzling French fried potatoes were lifted from boiling oil and clamped over the edge of the vat to drain. An unfamiliar country music tune blared from an overhead speaker.

Lillian pushed through the line of people waiting to be seated. She scanned the dining area. Karen was sitting in a booth near a back window. Lillian waved and hurried toward her. She dodged a waiter carrying a tray of dirty dishes and slid in the booth opposite Karen. "Hi, I'm sure glad you came early."

Karen nodded. "I went ahead and ordered the soup and salad specials for us."

"Fine." Karen's face was pale. Her auburn hair was pulled back and the ends turned under. Light from the window reflected off her hair in shiny auburn highlights.

"All set for your interview Monday? Oh, and I like your hair like that. It looks, umm, very business-like."

"Mo-om. I wear it this way half the time. And it looks terrible. I've got a hair appointment in the morning. Then I have to go shopping. By myself. Everyone else is too busy." She flattened her lips into a line.

Lillian shrugged, tried to keep her facial expression neutral. "You have a good sense of style. You don't need anyone to go with you."

Karen rolled her eyes.

The waiter appeared and plunked down their soup and salads. He was tall and skinny with longish sun-streaked brown hair. His dark eyes crinkled at the corners when he looked at Karen. "Get you guys anything else?"

Karen was staring out the window. Her cheeks were sucked in, forming shadowy hollows.

Lillian shook her head at the waiter and smiled. "No thanks. Just some time."

After the waiter left, Lillian stirred her soup. It was tomato with chopped-up parsley and cheese sprinkled over the top. "About the other night. I wanted to explain about the flying lessons. You see, I learned how to fly and—"

Karen's grey eyes darkened. "Mo-om. Would you just stop making up dumb excuses. I'm not a child. I know I don't need you to go shopping with me. I just thought it would be fun." She ripped the plastic wrap off a package of crackers. Bits of broken cracker scattered across the table and off the edge.

Lillian brushed aside some of the crumbs with her napkin and replaced the napkin in her lap. "Sweetie, I'm not making up anything. Honest. I taught myself how to fly. I'd like to show you. That would be better than explaining. Couldn't you at least come watch me do some of the demonstration before you went shopping? You wouldn't have to stay long. Also, I'd love to have you in my class. I'm not just trying to get out of going shopping with you. But flying is so important. It is—"

"And my interview isn't?" Karen glared at her.

"I didn't mean that and you know it." Lillian pressed her lips together. She'd better stop for now and try again later.

That evening several more people called about her newspaper ad, but none of them signed up. Lillian opened her flying school notebook and read the list of names: Robby Fulton, Marty Jones and the retired couple, Grace and George Wilson. Four students. But enough for a class. If anyone else called after tonight, they'd just have to wait until the next class.

Chapter 8
First Lesson

The next morning, Lillian woke up thirty minutes ahead of the alarm clock. She dashed to the window and pulled back the curtains. The clouds were pink and gold. Blue sky already showed. She sighed. A perfect day for flying.

Humming, she pulled on jeans and a heavy sweater then hurried into the kitchen. She flipped on the TV and listened to the news while she poured a glass brimful of orange juice and broke two eggs into a skillet.

She twirled around the kitchen on her tiptoes. Today, even all the storms and mean, dishonest people and terrible wars and other awful things happening all over the world couldn't spoil her happiness.

After breakfast she stacked her dishes in the sink, wiped off the counter, made up her bed and in minutes was in her car heading for the meadow.

Once there she pulled out a sheet of cardboard with LILLIAN'S FLYING SCHOOL printed on it in bold black letters. She thumbtacked the sign to a tree, then boosted herself up onto the hood of her car to sit.

Several minutes later a rusty blue van with palm trees and a sunset painted on the side rattled down the road and pulled in beside her. A teenaged boy with shoulder-length blonde hair got out. He wore faded jeans with frayed holes in the knees and a denim jacket. He shoved his hands deep in the pockets of his jacket as he slouched toward her.

Lillian jumped off the hood of her car and smiled at him. "Hi, you must be Robby Fulton?"

"Yeah." Robby shoved his hands deeper into his pockets. "You the one going to …?"

"Teach you how to fly?" Lillian said.

Robby shrugged. "Yeah. Where's the others? I mean, there are others coming aren't there?"

"Of course. Three more. But it's still early."

The Wilsons arrived next. Grace Wilson was wearing white sneakers, grey sweat pants and a white quilted down parka. A fringe of curly white hair showed under the hood of her parka. George Wilson had worn faded navy sneakers, grey sweat pants and a navy parka. Lillian waved at them. "Hello! You came!"

"Of course," Mrs. Wilson said, hurrying toward her. "We told you we would."

"I worried a little that you might change your minds."

50

Mr. Wilson grinned. "We figured it was worth a try. What could we possibly lose?"

Lillian smiled.

After introducing Robby and the Wilsons to each other, she suggested that they wait another five minutes more for the last person.

The time was almost up when an old blue sedan pulled in. A dark-haired woman and a blonde curly-haired little girl got out and walked toward them.

"I'm Marty Jones and this is Sally," the woman said. pulling up the hood of her quilted, khaki-colored jacket. She leaned over Sally, pulled the edges of her yellow jacket together at the bottom and zipped it up to her neck. She pulled up Sally's hood and tied it under her chin. She straightened and looked at Lillian.

"My husband had a business appointment this morning, and Sally was supposed to stay with a friend. But the friend got sick. I didn't want to leave her alone all morning. I hope it was all right to bring her," Marty said.

Sally hopped from one foot to the other, swinging her arms. She stood still and looked at Lillian. "Mommy said you're going to teach her how to fly? Can I too? I'm six."

Lillian smiled. "If it's all right with your mom. Actually, it might even be easier for you than for the rest of us."

"Why? Why?" Sally asked.

"Because children aren't so cluttered up with disbelief."

51

Lillian looked at the other students and smiled. "You'll understand better when I give the demonstration."

"It's fine with me," Marty said. "For Sally to fly. As long as you think it's safe for a child."

After introducing Marty and Sally to the others, Lillian led everyone away from the cars to the edge of the meadow. She turned and faced the group. "Watching me demonstrate flying is crucial. What I just said to Sally is true. In order to fly, you really do need to believe it's possible. Doubting will definitely slow your progress. It could even prevent you from flying altogether. Watching me fly should give you a big advantage over me. I predict that you will learn much faster than I did."

The students stood close together in a line while Lillian walked through the tall, spiky, brown grass toward the center of the meadow.

Her heart thudded against her ribs. She'd never flown in front of anyone. Would nervousness matter? Might it even keep her grounded? Her fingers inside her gloves grew icy. The inside of her mouth turned as dry as if she'd blotted it with a towel. She drew in a breath and held it. She exhaled and breathed in again.

In the middle of the meadow, Lillian stopped. She waved back at her students and looked around. Dew droplets sparkled like tiny crystal beads on the grass. The trees' bare branches formed dark silhouettes against the sky. Overhead, clouds were streaked with gold. Her students' excited voices drifted toward her.

Now. Now. Lillian tossed the ends of her red and white scarf over her shoulders. She drew in a long deep breath and stretched her arms straight up over her head.

She reached as high as she could, spreading her fingers wide apart. She paused. It was as if time had stopped, as if the meadow held its breath, as if even the sun stopped rising.

In a single motion, she then dropped her arms and stooped, bending forward until her forehead touched her knees. Then, like an uncoiling spring, she straightened, her toes pushing against the ground as she looked up between her arms. Her entire body strained upward. Nothing could have held her to the ground. Nothing.

She zoomed straight up, higher and higher, the air rushing past her, whipping out the ends of her scarf and wisps of reddish hair that had escaped from her stocking cap.

Finally, high above the meadow, Lillian lowered her arms and leveled her body parallel to the ground. Far below, her students looked like dolls. She waved at them, then flew into an upward air current and let it carry her in spirals still higher.

For a minute or two, she rolled onto her back and drifted on air currents. But then she flipped back onto her stomach and flew back and forth above the meadow as fast as she could. She loved to feel the air rushing past her face, her body, her legs, to feel every muscle straining to its limit.

53

Finally, pressing her arms against her sides, she dived straight down. The air shrieked past her ears and her eyes teared.

At the last moment, just before crashing into the tree tops, she leveled her body. She circled the meadow once and landed on her feet in front of her students.

Robby shook his head. "Wow! Awesome!"

"Oh, teach me, teach me!" Sally said, clapping her hands and jumping up and down. "Please, please, teach me how to fly."

George Wilson took off his glasses and rubbed his eyes. "I can't believe it! I've seen it, but I still can't believe it!"

Grace Wilson squeezed George Wilson's arm. "It's truly wonderful, but we haven't been exercising the way we're supposed to."

"Oh," Marty Jones said. "You did fly. And you think I can too? It isn't a trick, is it?"

Lillian smiled. "No. You can believe your eyes." One at a time, she looked closely at each student. "Now do you really want to learn how? Because you won't be able to unless you want to do this more than anything else in the world. It will take almost all the energy you have."

Nobody spoke. All five students stared at Lillian, their eyes wide and anxious.

Lillian clapped her hands and blew on them. "Maybe you should think about it until next Saturday? Then if you still want to learn how, come back. Same time, and we'll begin at once. We'll take it in stages. I promise not to expect you to do anything you can't."

Except for Sally, the students said little as they walked back to their cars.

Sally skipped beside her mother. "Oh, goody, I'm going to learn how! I don't have to think about it."

Marty touched her shoulder. "Shhh. You're just a child. There may be more to this than you realize."

"I agree," Mr. Wilson said.

Mrs. Wilson nodded. "What if I do something wrong and crash?"

Robby pulled open the van's door. "She said she'd do it in stages."

Lillian watched her students getting into their cars and waved. Would they come back? At least some of them?

Chapter 9
Family Problems

The next week Lillian went to work as usual and in free moments wondered about her students. Would they come back? Or not? There was so much she wanted to teach them. So much to share.

When Saturday morning finally arrived, fog covered everything. Her car, parked in front of her apartment, was barely visible. Should she call her students and tell them the weather wouldn't matter? No. If they let a little fog stop them, the desire to fly wouldn't be strong enough. That inner longing was crucial to give them enough lift.

Robby was sitting in his van, when she arrived at the meadow. He rolled down the side window as she pulled in beside him.

Lillian got out of her car and walked toward him. "You came back!" she said, jamming her red and white stocking hat down over her ears. "Does that mean ...?"

Robby nodded. "Yeah, I want to learn how. But my dad almost wouldn't let me come." He pulled a folded sheet of paper out of his jacket pocket and handed it to Lillian. "Here's the permission slip."

"But he gave his permission."

"It's not that," Robby murmured. He was going to ground me because of my report card. He said anything was better than me wasting time with my friends. He said I'll never amount to anything, if I don't straighten up."

"Oh." Lillian looked at him. She looped the ends of her scarf around her neck another time.

"Yeah. But I might drop out of school. I'm sixteen. I could move out, get a job." He looked down, clenching the steering wheel with both hands.

Lillian nodded. She traced the window edge with her finger. He was hurt and angry. But now wasn't the time to get into that. It was almost time for the class to start. The others should be arriving any moment if they were coming. "Anyway, I'm glad you came back. Really glad. I hope the others will."

Robby looked at her, his eyes anxious. "If they don't, could you still teach me? Do you have to have the others?"

"No," she said softly. "I don't have to have any certain number. It'd just be nice to have a group."

A car turned around the bend in the road. In the fog, it was barely visible.

"It's Marty Jones," Lillian said, as the car approached, "and Sally!"

58

Marty parked beside Robby's van. She and Sally got out and hurried toward Lillian. Sally's eyes opened wide. "Now can we start?"

"Calm down," Marty said, grabbing her hand.

"I'm excited too," Lillian said, "and Sally, I'm glad you and your mom came back."

Sally grinned. "Daddy got mad. He said we're just making it up. He said if we learned how to fly, it'd save on gas money. He said we might need to because business is slow."

"Sally's right," Marty said. "He wouldn't even listen when I tried to explain. I said he could come and watch. He said he had to look up all the outstanding accounts. He's worried if they don't pay up we might have to declare bankruptcy. I told him it's not that bad. I know because I do the books."

"Maybe he just needs time to adjust to you pursuing a new interest," Lillian said. An image of Karen's angry face surfaced in her mind. "I'm sure he will manage. But right now is your time to do something that's important to you. Do you want to fly? Deep down really want to?"

"Yes," Marty said, squeezing Sally's hand. "I don't know if I can, but I want to try."

"Good." Lillian glanced at her watch. "Let's wait a few more minutes for the Wilsons."

She'd almost given up when they arrived.

"Sorry, we're late," Mr. Wilson said, shoving up the collar on his parka. "We got to talking over our coffee and time got away from us."

Mrs. Wilson nodded. "Do you know? We've talked about flying all week. We've hardly talked about anything else."

Mr. Wilson swung his arms. "Grace's right. I mean here I am seventy-nine years old, and I'm like a kid about this." He paused. "You really don't think we're too old? I don't get around like I used to."

Lillian laughed. "Of course you're not too old! Age doesn't matter. Like I told you last week, we'll take it in stages, and any time you think I'm going too fast, all you have to do is tell me and I'll be happy to slow down."

A dreamy look came over Mrs. Wilson's face. "Oh, just think how it would be to fly over the trees beside our apartment building and look down into a bird's nest and see the babies up close."

"And can't you imagine Evie Tilson's face," Mr. Wilson said, "if we just happened to fly past her window and she and Mr. Tilson looked out and saw us?" He doubled over, laughing.

"Who's Mrs. Tilson?" Sally asked.

"A very proper lady," Mr. Wilson said, "who lives in the condo over us. She disapproves of anyone who doesn't act exactly the way she thinks they should."

Sally grabbed her mother's arm. "I want to see her face too! Let's all fly past their window. Can we? Can we?"

Marty frowned at her. "Mr. Wilson didn't really mean they were really going to. He was just...." She glared at him.

60

Mr. Wilson hunched his shoulders. "I didn't mean to start something. But Evie always makes me feel like she's just caught me doing something wrong."

"Like my dad," Robby said. "He doesn't approve of anything I do either."

"All right," Lillian said, waving her arms. "Now that everyone's here, let's begin."

The students followed Lillian to the meadow. She pointed at two long tree trunks lying in grass at the edge of the clearing. "You can sit on those."

The students sat next to each other in a row and looked up at her.

She clapped her gloved hands together. Even with gloves on, her fingers were still cold. "First of all, I am so very glad that all of you came back. This is going to be an adventure—for me as well as you. "Before we get started, I want to go over a few things."

Holding her hands behind her back, Lillian crossed her fingers. Flying was so important. So much she wanted to teach it to her students. "First, it's important to eat a well-balanced diet. Plenty of fruits and vegetables. And get some exercise every day, even if it's just a walk around the block at first."

She looked into her students' eyes and paused. "Also, find some time every day, when you won't be interrupted, to do nothing but concentrate on flying. Sit in a comfortable position, relax and close your eyes. Then imagine that tiny moment of weight-lessness at the height of a jump. Try to lengthen that moment. Imagine your body becoming light as a cotton ball, all your bones hollow and filled with air. And over and over, think the words, 'I can fly, I can fly' and 'nothing can stop me.' The more you believe it is possible for you to fly, the easier it will be. Believe me."

"Now everyone stand up. I'm going to teach you how to prepare to jump. You will need to practice this and the other steps every day."

Marty gripped Sally's hand. "You're sure this is safe for a child?"

"Of course," Lillian said. "But you'll have to let go of her hand." She looked at her students and took a breath. "All right, everyone, spread out."

The students stepped away from each other, forming a wide semi-circle in front of Lillian.

"Perfect," Lillian said. "Now, stand as tall and straight as you can, and raise your arms over your heads."

She stepped back and observed. "Straighten your elbows, Mr. Wilson. Robby, you need to bring your shoulders in closer to your head." She smiled. "Everyone's looking good! Very good! Now reach for a cloud. There you go!"

"Now, up on your tiptoes, and at the same time, look up at the sky."

Everyone stumbled except for Sally.

"I'm too out of shape, " Mr. Wilson said.

"Maybe we really are too old," said Mrs. Wilson.

"Nonsense," Lillian said. "That was only your first attempt. "Come on. Let's try again."

62

The students rearranged themselves in front of Lillian. On the third try, Robby succeeded, and on the fifth try so did Marty and the Wilsons.

"Now the next step," Lillian said. "Watch me first." She rose onto her tiptoes. "Take a deep breath, then bring your arms down to your sides. Next, stoop close as you can to the ground. If possible, put your hands flat on the ground."

She stood. "All right, let's try it!"

Half-way down, Mrs. Wilson stopped. "I can't go down any farther."

"Me neither," Mr. Wilson said.

"Doesn't matter for now." Lillian said. "With practice you'll be able to stoop farther. You only need to go down far enough to be able to spring back up."

After they'd practiced this step several times Lillian waved her arms. "Now we're going to add the springing up motion. This is where you get the lift to leave the ground."

Lillian stooped to the ground. "As you rise," she said, slowly standing and lifting her arms, "look up at the sky. At the same time, fling your arms up over your head, rise onto the balls of your feet, press your feet against the ground and push hard with your toes."

Robby and Sally did it the first time, but Marty and the Wilsons kept losing their balance.

"Let's take a break?" Lillian said. "We've been at this a good while."

Her students followed her to the same two tree trunks. Lillian sat down, loosened her scarf from around her neck, and stretched out her legs in front of her. The Wilsons and Marty sat beside her.

"Can I go walking?" Sally asked her mother.

Robby stepped behind her. "If you want, I'll go with her?"

Marty hesitated. "All right. But not too far."

As Robby and Sally headed across the meadow, Marty said, "I almost said 'no.' But. I don't know. He seems all right."

George Wilson nodded. "It's probably the long hair and driving that beat-up van."

Grace Wilson laughed. "I still remember your ponytail and how upset my grandmother was the first time she met you?"

"But it was a short one. And once swim team practice started back up, I had to cut it off."

Lillian smiled. She wiggled her toes inside her sneakers. "Basically, I think Robby's just a very sensitive teen who's trying hard not to let that show."

She looked beyond the cars and up the graveled road. The fog was lifting. Overhead were patches of blue sky. And all of her students had come back. This had to be the most amazing thing she'd ever experienced.

After a few more minutes, Lillian suggested that she work with just Marty and the Wilsons since Robby and Sally already could do the moves.

"Well," Mrs. Wilson said after she finally succeeded. "Maybe I can learn to fly after all."

Mr. Wilson grinned. "Same here."

64

"You know this is fun," Marty said. Several strands of dark hair had worked out of her wool cap and fallen across her cheek. She shoved the hair back in place. "Even if we weren't learning how to fly, it's still fun being out here with everyone."

A few minutes later, Robby and Sally returned.

"We went in the woods," Sally said. "But this woods isn't as big as the one behind my school. We walked all the way to the other side. You can't do that in the woods at my school. My teacher won't let us even go in them. She said we might get lost. Besides it's private property."

"That sounds sensible," Marty said. She smiled at Robby. "Thank you for going with her. While you and Sally were gone, we learned how to do that springing up part."

"Yep," Mr. Wilson said. "Guess we caught up with you young'uns."

Robby's face turned red. He looked down. "I'm glad you caught on."

"Robby's nice," Sally said. "He taught me how to whistle. You put your thumb and finger in your mouth and blow." Like this. She put her thumb and finger in her mouth and blew, making a shrill whistle.

Mr. Wilson laughed. "When I was a kid, growing up on a farm, I had a horse I called by whistling like that."

"Well," Lillian said, "our time's up for this week. Does everyone remember what to practice?"

All five nodded.

"Then goodbye, and I'll see you next Saturday."

On the way home, Lillian sang her made-up flying song and tapped out the rhythm on the steering wheel. She just knew something wonderful was about to happen.

Chapter 10
First Flight

The next Saturday when Lillian arrived at the meadow, her students were already there, talking and warming up.

Sally waved. "Hi, Ms. Lillian. We beat you!"

"You sure did!" Lillian said, warmth spreading inside her.

Mr. Wilson grinned. "You wouldn't believe how we've looked forward to this. We practiced, and I can stoop almost to the ground! I haven't felt this good in years!"

"Me either," Mrs. Wilson said. "I even pulled out my old mandolin from the back of my closet. I bought a new set of strings, and I've started playing it again."

"And that sure got Evie Tilson riled up," said Mr. Wilson. He grinned.

Mrs. Wilson nodded. "She was in the elevator yesterday. She said, 'Where were you, yesterday? You missed the monthly meeting of the Descendants of the Green Valley Founding Fathers and didn't tell anyone.' Then she looked at my mandolin case and said, 'What on earth is that guitar-looking case you're carrying?' I just smiled and said, 'It's a mandolin case. And I'm sure no one missed me at the meeting. I'd planned to go, but I was practicing and forgot the time.' And then would you believe it? Evie puffed up and said, 'Well, be sure you don't miss the next meeting. There was talk about nominating you as an officer for next year.'"

Mr. Wilson put his arm around Mrs. Wilson's shoulders and hugged her to his side. "My dear Gracie said, 'Evie, please whatever you do, don't nominate me for anything. I simply can't do anything more."

Mrs. Wilson nodded. "Then Evie pressed her lips together, gave me a squinty-eyed look and didn't say another word."

"She's like my dad," Robby said. "He's always on me about something. If it wasn't for coming here, I was thinking I might take off, go to California or somewhere."

Lillian looked at him. "You said something like this last week."

Robby shrugged. He glanced at the others, then at the ground. He scuffed the toe of his sneaker and kicked a pebble. When he spoke his voice was so quiet that Lillian barely made out the words. "My dad said I'm probably going to end up in jail." He looked up and glared at Lillian. "It'd serve him right if I did."

Before Lillian could respond, Mrs. Wilson, said, "Oh, Robby."

Mr. Wilson put his hand on Robby's shoulder. "What's the matter, son?"

Lillian smiled at Robby. Whatever the problem, it wasn't just going to disappear. "That hurts, doesn't it, hearing your dad say things like that?"

Robby nodded. "Only it's not just talking, it's yelling too."

Sally's eyes filled with tears and she reached for Marty's hand.

The Wilsons and Marty exchanged glances. They looked at Lillian. Lillian nodded and looked back at Robby.

"You said your dad was always on you about something? Do you want to give an example?"

Robby looked around the circle of students then back at the ground. "My homework."

"Your dad yells at you a lot about your homework?"

"Yeah," Robby said, "The principal told him my teachers said I wasn't doing my homework."

"Is that true?"

Robby nodded. He twisted a button on his jacket then shoved his hands deep into the pockets of his jeans.

"Hmmm." Lillian pulled off her knit cap and gloves. She ran her fingers through her hair. This might backfire. But he seemed to trust her and to want very much to fly. She spoke softly. "Would it help if we came up with a plan to make your dad stop giving you such a hard time?"

Robby shrugged. He looked at her, chewed his lower lip.

Lillian looked across the meadow at the trees that edged it, at a plume of smoke from a distant chimney. She looked back at Robby. "I've got an idea. But it's kind of obvious. Want to hear it?"

Robby shrugged again.

Lillian pulled on her cap, drawing it down over her ears. She slid her fingers back into her gloves. "Of course, I don't know your dad, so I can't promise anything. But it sure wouldn't make things any worse." She paused, again. "What if you just did your homework and handed it in on time without waiting for your dad or anyone to remind you?"

Robby's face turned red. He glared at Lillian then looked down and scuffed the toe of one sneaker on top of the other.

She grinned. "And what about your teachers? What do you think they'd do?"

Robby glanced at Lillian. His lips curved slightly. "They'd die of shock. Anyway, you're making fun of me!"

"Maybe it is a little funny," Lillian said, "and you think so too. I saw you smile. Seriously, I guess I'm wondering if one reason your dad's giving you a hard time is because he thinks having an education is important. I doubt your dad and your teachers and the principal would bother if they didn't care about you."

Robby glared. "Well, I don't care about them. Anyway, it wouldn't work." He kicked a pebble. It skittered into the tall grass and disappeared. He kicked another pebble.

Lillian shrugged. "What have you got to lose? Might be worth a try, like an experiment, to see what would happen. Maybe just until next week?"

Robby kicked another rock. "My friends would think I was trying to be good. They'd stop liking me."

Mr. Wilson huffed his breath. "If they stopped liking you for doing the right thing, I wouldn't consider them friends. If they say anything, you just tell me who they are. I'll give them a piece of my mind!"

"Please, Robby," Sally said, "Do what Ms. Lillian says. I want you to come back."

Marty pulled Sally to her side. "You stay out of it."

Lillian waved her arms. "All right, everyone. Let's go learn how to fly

The students followed Lillian to the middle of the meadow. "First," she said, "let's go through the steps you learned last week. Did everyone practice?"

"Every chance I got," Marty said. "I even did them to music."

"And I drew a picture about flying," Sally said. "Want to see it? It's in the car."

"Of course," Lillian said. "But let's wait until after our lesson." She raised her voice. "Everyone spread out."

"Very good!" Lillian said after they'd gone through all the steps. "I can tell you've been working. Now there's one more thing I must teach you before you actually fly. How to land."

She stood straight and tall, lifting the back of her head. She rolled back her shoulders a couple of times, relaxing them. "The important thing about landing is always to flex your knees. They'll be like the shock absorbers on a car. Here, I'll show you."

Lillian climbed onto a rock and jumped. As she landed, her knees bent then straightened. "All right. Now it's your turn."

One by one the students jumped off the rock, and Lillian nodded and smiled.

"Now a couple of practice jumps," she said, "and you'll be ready to fly."

The students spread out and stood onto their tiptoes, then stooped and jumped several inches into the air.

Lillian clapped her hands. "You're beautiful! Let's do one more!"

They jumped again.

Lillian's heart rocketed inside her chest. They'd caught on so fast, she could hardly believe it. And each lesson was more fun than the one before. Whoever could have dreamed life could be this exciting, this exhilarating?

"All right, now the next time when you jump, I want you to think the words, 'I'm going up, up, up, nothing can stop me.' Think them over and over. Jump

72

as high as you possibly can, and always remember to imagine weightlessness. We'll jump together. And when I say, 'level off,' lean forward."

She pointed across the meadow. "Aim for that tall pine tree with the broken-off branch. No higher than that branch. Right before you get there, turn around, come back here and land."

"What if I forget something?" Mrs. Wilson asked.

"We won't be that high," Lillian said. "But if you do fall, just duck your head and roll."

Her students stood on their tiptoes and raised their arms.

"Remember. Keep thinking, 'I can fly, I can fly,'" Lillian said. "Now, deep breaths, everyone. Ready! Stoop! Jump!"

The ground dropped beneath Lillian and her students as they jumped. Their arms stretched out straight over their heads. Their legs were together, their bodies straight as arrows. Their jackets, caps, and scarves were splashes of color against the sky.

"Level out!" Lillian yelled when they had reached the height of the broken off branch. "You're high enough!"

Everyone leaned forward. Only Mr. Wilson leaned too far and began falling.

"Raise your arms. Look up!" Lillian shouted at him.

"Now everyone, move forward! Keep moving!" she shouted again as she headed across the meadow, "so you won't fall."

Robby kicked his legs as if he were swimming. He almost bumped into Mr. Wilson because he was flying so fast.

"I'm flying! I'm flying!" Robby called out.

"I did it!" Mrs. Wilson said, breathing unevenly as she flew past in a slightly jerky zigzag pattern. "I did it!"

"Wheee!" Sally yelled, waving both arms.

Mr. Wilson shouted, "Whoever would believe it? Who'd ever believe I could do something like this?"

Tears blew off Marty's cheeks when she flew beside Lillian. "Thank you for this. How can I ever thank you enough?"

After they had flown all the way across the meadow and back, they landed and crowded around Lillian.

"That was wonderful!" Mrs. Wilson said. "Let's do it again, only this time go higher!"

"Yes," everyone said, their voices eager.

"I've never felt so good in my whole life!" Mr. Wilson said.

Sally clapped her hands. "Me too. I want to fly again too!"

Robby nodded.

"Very well," Lillian said. "We still have time. But no higher than the tree tops."

This time the students waved and called to each other as they swooped back and forth above the meadow. Sometimes their toes and fingers touched the bare, top-most branches of the trees.

Sally and Robby chased each other, playing flying tag. Mrs. Wilson rolled from her stomach to her back to her stomach over and over. George Wilson somersaulted backwards.

Finally Lillian waved and pointed at the ground. "Time's up!"

On the way to their cars, Lillian walked beside Sally. "Now I want to see your picture." She called to the others. "Is there anything we need to talk about before leaving?"

They all shook their heads.

As Marty opened the door on the driver's side of her car and slid behind the steering wheel, Sally lifted her picture off the back seat. In the picture, a stick figure with yellow curly hair was flying across a blue sky. "That's me," said Sally.

"It's a wonderful picture," Lillian said.

"You can have it," Sally said. She grinned as she climbed into the front seat of the car beside her mother. She rolled down the window. "When I get home I'm going to show Daddy I really can fly! Now, he'll believe us!"

Lillian's breath caught. "Be sure to tell him first." But Marty had already started the car and was backing into the road.

Chapter 11
Lillian Runs into Sylvia

On the way home, Lillian stopped by the grocery store to pick up milk and a bag of oranges. Inside the store Sylvia Jeffers was leaning over the meat counter. "Hi," Lillian said rushing toward her. "Am I ever glad to have run into you."

Sylvia turned around. She held a package of plastic-wrapped ground-beef patties in each hand. Her eyes opened wide. "Lillian. How are you? I'd about given up on ever seeing you again."

"I know, and it's mostly my fault." Lillian opened her handbag and fished around inside it. She pulled out her cell phone and touched the calendar app with the tip of her finger. "Right now before we talk anymore, let's schedule a time to get together."

"All right, but it'll have to be on a weekend."

"Mm mm. I know. I try to turn in early on weeknights too." Lillian checked the schedule on her phone. "I'm pretty tied up Saturday mornings. What about this coming Sunday afternoon?"

"Ed and I always go to a movie on Sundays."

"Every Sunday?"

"We've been going to a marriage counselor. We're trying to do more things together. That's about the only time we're both free."

Lillian stared at her phone. She really didn't want to do anything more on Saturdays after flying all morning. But she didn't want to lose Sylvia's friendship either. "What about this coming Saturday around 1:00? We could meet for lunch. That would give me time to get back from what I have scheduled that morning."

Sylvia smiled. "Perfect. Ed has to work most of this Saturday. You know, I was beginning to think you'd dropped Ed and me."

Lillian shook her head. "Never. You two are my oldest, closest friends."

Sylvia ran her tongue over her lips. "Listen, we've got a neighborhood potluck tonight so I've got to run. But one quick thing. The whole neighborhood is talking about it. Your ex just had another run-in with Theodore and Agnes. It's a hoot. Fill you in Saturday."

She threw her arms around Lillian and hugged her. "The old neighborhood still misses you. Remember the get-togethers at your house? How you'd play the piano and everyone would stand around and sing?"

Chapter 12
Karen Relays Information

Lillian smiled as she drove home from the grocery store. What on earth had Michael done this time to upset the Greens? Let his dog turn over their garbage can again? Whatever, it was no concern of hers.

Their marriage was over. That ended on the day he walked out, abandoning her and seven-year-old Karen. She'd grieved for years. No more. She was over him. Finished. It would be good to catch up with Sylvia over a leisurely lunch as well as good to have a chance to explain flying and its importance.

When Lillian pulled into her apartment complex parking lot, Karen's red car was parked in front of Lillian's apartment. Lillian parked beside the car and took out her groceries from the trunk of the car. She heard piano music.

Inside the apartment, Karen was sitting at Lillian's upright piano. She was wearing black tights

79

and a blue turtleneck sweater. A mug of hot chocolate sat, untouched, on a coaster on the coffee table beside two dress boxes. Karen lifted her hands from the piano keys and turned toward Lillian

"I see you did go shopping," Lillian said, unwinding her scarf and pulling off her cap. She unbuttoned her coat, slipped it over a hanger and hung the hanger over a rod in the closet.

Karen frowned. "For the second time. Bryant Securities called back. I've got a second interview on Monday. I got lucky. Suits were on sale." She opened one of the boxes and took out a grey flannel jacket. She held it up. "I thought this looked conservative enough."

Lillian ran her fingers down the front of the jacket. "It's lovely. Very businesslike. Why don't you model it for me? Then I want to explain about the flying lessons. It's past time you knew—"

Karen's dark eyes flashed. "Mom, please be serious. You haven't acted like yourself in weeks."

"Honey, I *am* serious. It's—"

Karen held out the palm of her hand toward Lillian. "Anyway, I don't have time for a fashion show. I've got to wash my hair and get ready to go out." She started folding the jacket then paused. "I almost forgot. Dad dropped by the other night and we went to LITTLE CHICK'S."

She looked down and drew in a breath. "He said he and my stepmom are getting a divorce. He asked if you were seeing anyone."

Lillian shook her head. "Honey, don't. Your dad and I are over. But that reminds me, I just ran into Sylvia at the store. She said your dad and Theodore got into a tiff of some kind. I'm curious. She didn't have time to tell me what about. Did your dad say anything to you?"

Karen sighed. "I don't know why you haven't heard. Everyone's been talking about it. Mr. Green's short-haired pointer show dog had this litter of puppies that he was so proud of. Until the vet told him the puppies looked like a Golden Retriever mix. Mr. Green was furious. He claimed the sire was Ranger. Dad told him he should be more careful that his dog didn't get out, and besides there was more than one Golden Retriever in town."

Lillian shook her head.

"Mo—om, it's just a stupid nothing. Won't you at least think about giving Dad another chance?" Karen folded in the sleeves of the jacket and laid it back in the box.

She gathered up the boxes and stood. "I told him it was all right to call you. I said I thought you were lonely. Well, I've got to go now." She pursed her lips slightly as she stood and walked toward the door.

Lillian frowned. "I wish you hadn't done that. Said he could call. And what makes you think I'm lonely? Please don't rush off."

"I'm not. I've already been here a long time waiting on you. And I should've brought some music. Not everyone plays by ear."

"Good luck on Monday," Lillian called as Karen opened the door and stepped onto the porch.

Chapter 13
The Jones' Crisis

On Monday morning, as Lillian walked out the door to go to work, her cell phone rang. It was Marty Jones.

"Harry and I had a big fight," she sobbed. "He told me to stop flying and said if Sally ever even mentioned it, she'd stay in her room for a month." She sniffed. "Excuse me."

Lillian heard rattling as if Marty's phone was being set on a table. This was followed by muffled snuffling. "I said he was overreacting," Marty continued, "and I said I wouldn't stop flying. He got angry and said, 'Well I might not be able to stop you, but I'll see to it that Sally never flies again!'"

"What happened?" Lillian asked. Her stomach muscles tightened. "But we can't talk long. I've got an early appointment. If we don't have time to finish, call me at the office, or I can call you after work." She unzipped the neck of her parka several inches.

Marty sniffed. "It was on Saturday after our lesson. Sally was so excited. She couldn't wait to show Harry. But you'd think she'd committed a crime.

"She flew across the living room one time and he yelled, 'Stop that!' It scared her so badly that she fell and crashed into the coffee table. She cut her lip and bruised her face and both legs. We had to take her to the emergency room to get her lip stitched. When we got back home, she went back to her room in tears. Then someone from Child Protective Services came out and talked to us."

Lillian ran her tongue over her dry lips.

"Harry said I never should've answered your ad—that everything was fine before that. I said he shouldn't have yelled at Sally. He said it was my fault for letting her learn how to fly. Then he walked outside, slammed the door, and didn't come home until 2 a.m."

Lillian looked out the window. Bare tree branches were bending in the wind. A utility truck rolled past in the street, throwing icy slush against the curb. "He was probably shocked to see Sally fly," she managed, but her words came out a little thin. "You said he hadn't believed flying was possible?"

There was a long pause, then Marty said," Well, I'm not giving it up. I sat up all night thinking what to do. And Sally's miserable. She moped around the house all yesterday, and she didn't want to go to school today. She's never been this unhappy for so long. She begged me to talk her father into letting her keep flying. But Harry and I aren't even speaking. If this keeps on, I'll take Sally and leave!"

Lillian gripped the phone. "Marty, I want you to listen to me! Don't do anything right now that you may regret later. There isn't time now but we need to talk more."

Marty sobbed. "'Oh, Lillian, I don't know what to do. I really don't want to leave Harry but I want to fly too, and so does Sally."

At work, after her first client had left, Lillian checked her phone and found a text message. "Please call at once. Karen."

Now what? Lillian's finger trembled as she placed the call.

Karen picked up after the first ring. "Mom, I'm at the gift shop, but it's quiet right now and I had to tell you. You'll never believe it. Never. I got the job! I mean I have to get in a training program first. But isn't it fantastic? I start tomorrow. The gift shop's almost overstaffed because of the economy being slow, and they said I can leave whenever I want to. Can you meet me at the mall after work to celebrate? I'll buy you a pizza! Isn't it wonderful! Karen Brown, stockbroker!"

Tears filled Lillian's eyes "Congratulations, sweetie. I'm so happy for you. And I'd love to meet you for pizza." She drew in a deep breath as she laid down the phone. What a relief. Now, hopefully, they could start talking without arguing over the least little thing.

Chapter 14
Lillian Meets Karen at the Mall

It was almost dark when Lillian walked inside the mall. Karen stood in front of the large, glass-covered directory. She was wearing a long, black quilted coat with a hood rimmed in some kind of fur. Lillian assumed it was fake. The hood was pulled back on her shoulders, nestling her shiny auburn hair.

"Hi, Mom," Karen said, rushing to Lillian and throwing her arms around her.

Lillian hugged Karen to her. "Honey, I'm so happy for you. I can't wait to hear about your job."

"It's a dream come true," Karen said, pulling away. She motioned down the mall toward a central area ringed with booths that offered food from different countries. "Come on. I'll tell you on the way. I'm starving." They walked toward the booths. "... I mean I liked the gift shop all right, especially the people, but well, it's just wasn't me. You know what I mean?"

"Of course. That why I keep trying to tell you about flying."

"Mo—om." Karen stopped and grabbed Lillian's arm, shook it a little. "Please don't ruin tonight."

Lillian pulled her arm away. "Honey, I'm sorry, I didn't mean. Never mind. This is your celebration. I just keep getting carried away whenever I… but I do know the feeling you were talking about. Believe me."

Inside the food court they stopped in front of Fine Italian Foods and ordered slices of pizza with everything and chilled cans of soda. They carried their trays of food to a bench beside a fountain with revolving colored lights trained on it.

The water burbled, sending up a rainbow-colored mist. Tall, potted tropical plants surrounding the fountain gave off a damp, mossy, leafy odor. Lillian and Karen took off their coats and draped them over the back of the bench. They sat beside their coats, balancing the trays on their laps.

"My job's going to be wonderful," Karen said between mouthfuls of pizza. "Everyone's super. Mr. Bryant, he's the big boss, said he thinks I'll be a real asset to the company. I'll be like an intern sort of at first."

Karen stood up, set her tray down on the bench, and wiped her hands with a paper napkin. She smoothed down her grey flannel jacket and pants and turned completely around.

"How do think my outfit looks? Is the fit all right? I didn't have time to try it on for you Saturday." She frowned slightly.

"The fit looks perfect. And your suit is lovely. You look very professional."

"Thanks." Karen picked up her tray and sat back down. "But I have to buy some more suits. Bryant's is very proper, very traditional." She pressed her lips together as she poked a straw through the hole in the top of her can of soda.

Lillian held her breath, let it out slowly. "Do you wish I were more—traditional?"

Karen pursed her lips a moment, then bit off another mouthful of pizza.

Lillian nodded. "Anyway, I'm glad you're happy about your new job."After eating one pizza slice, she offered her other to Karen.

Karen scooted the pizza onto her plate. "I meant to tell you. When I was talking to Dad the other night? I didn't tell him about—your Saturdays."

"You could've, I wouldn't have minded."

"Mo-om."

"Lillian! Ms. Lillian!"

Lillian looked around. Robby Fulton was waving as he and a tall dark-haired man walked toward her and Karen.

"Hi," Robby said, stepping in front of Lillian. "This is my dad."

"Charles Fulton," the man said. He looked at Lillian intently as he held out his hand.

Lillian hastily wiped her fingers on a napkin and shook Charles's hand. It was firm and warm. "Glad to meet you. And this is my daughter Karen. We're celebrating her new job with Bryant Securities."

"Congratulations," Charles said to Karen. "I'm an attorney, and Bryant Securities is a block down the street from our law offices. They're easily the most prestigious brokerage firm in Green Valley." He looked back at Lillian.

"I have to say that what you are teaching is sure preferable to some of the activities that Robby has been pursuing. Really amazing," Charles continued. "Yesterday, I watched him fly around the back yard. It looked like fun."

Karen's eyes widened. She sucked in her cheeks.

Lillian smiled. "It is pretty amazing," She looked at Karen. "Robby is one of my flying students."

Karen drew her lips into a line. Without speaking, she stood, set her tray on the bench, picked up her coat and shook it out.

Charles stared at Karen, frowning slightly. "Sorry to have interrupted. Well, we better be getting on. Nice meeting you both. Come on, Robby."

Lillian watched them walk away. They seemed to be getting along. Good. But what about Marty's family? She hadn't heard from Marty since her morning phone call.

She looked back at Karen. Karen had put on her coat and was hurriedly buttoning it. "Honey, what is it? We've barely started talking."

"Mom, honestly. As if you didn't already know. I'm going home."

"But I keep trying to tell you about flying. It's not fair that you won't even listen to—"

Karen shook her head, flinging her long, straight auburn hair from side to side. She sat back down on the bench beside Lillian. "Mom, what is it with you? When I saw Mrs. Jeffers the other day, she said she hadn't seen you since the town meeting. She said you keep promising to call and you never do, and the times she called you, you always had an excuse why you couldn't meet her."

"And now this Robby Fulton and his father? They're weird. Really. Mom, I'm worried about you."

Lillian shook her head. "Don't be. At least let me bring you up to date on one thing, I just saw Sylvia a couple of days ago, and we're meeting for lunch on Saturday. Now why won't you at least give me a chance to tell you about flying?"

"Give up, Mom," Sylvia stood up, pulled up the hood of her coat and headed toward the mall exit doors. The slender high heels of her leather boots clicked angrily on the polished tiled floor.

Chapter 15
Charles Phones Lillian

On Tuesday morning, during a lull at work, Lillian called Marty Jones. Marty said that she and Harry still weren't speaking, and he was now sleeping on the sofa in the living room. She also said Sally's teacher had called to say that Sally wasn't paying attention in class and kept staring out the window at the sky.

Lillian offered to talk with Harry about flying. Marty said she doubted he'd be willing to.

That evening Lillian had just cleaned up the kitchen and was settling down in front of the television to listen to the news when her cell phone rang. It was Charles Fulton.

"Lillian? Sorry to bother you." His speech was abrupt. "What's all this talk about the flying lessons?"

"The flying lessons? I don't understand. Robby? Is he all right?"

"Robby's fine. Upset a little is all."

"What happened? Would you like to explain?" Lillian heard what sounded like a chair leg scraping the floor.

"This afternoon," Charles said," before I came home, Robby said Theodore Green came out here and said he was on town council business. Robby said he asked a lot of questions about the flying lessons. Who was teaching them? What they were doing in the classes? How long it had been going on? Things like that. Robby was quite upset by his visit. I called Theodore at home and left a message for him to call me. So far he hasn't. I promise you this: he won't get away with intimidating my son."

After ending the call, Lillian walked into the kitchen. She filled the kettle with water, set it on the stove top burner and turned on the heat. Her neck muscles ached. Maybe a cup of herbal tea would help relax them. Why were the flying lessons any concern of Theodore Green and the town council anyway?

Chapter 16
Theodore Green Visits Lillian

All day Wednesday, whenever the phone rang in the office, Lillian's first thought was, is it something concerning Charles Fulton and Theodore Green? But the calls all turned out to be from clients either wanting to speak to her, one of the other counselors or Will Hawkins.

Finally, she pulled out her "Do Not Disturb" sign, and between clients, hung the sign over the doorknob outside her office door. She then flew around her office, clearing her mind of all the negative thoughts she was having.

At last the work day ended. When Lillian drove toward her usual parking place in front of her apartment, she blinked. Theodore Green was standing on the cement walkway in front of her door. He had pulled down the ear flaps on his brown felt hat. His black hair that stuck out in front was plastered to his forehead. His long, brown overcoat was buttoned to his neck.

"Lillian. Lillian Brown!" he shouted as soon as she stepped out of her car.

Lillian stood beside her car a moment. "Yes? Give me a moment." Stepping carefully to avoid ice on the edges of the steps, she inched her way up the steps from the parking lot and onto the walkway.

Theodore Green peered down at her through his rimless glasses. "I'm here on official business. I have a serious matter to discuss with you. But we'd best go inside. I've been here awhile."

"Certainly." Lillian said. Her fingers trembled as she fumbled the key into the lock on her door. "You must be freezing."

Once inside, she waited until Theodore Green unbuttoned his coat, took it off, folded it neatly into a square and seated himself on the sofa. She sat in her lavender-flowered easy chair that was against the narrow wall space between the sofa and door.

Theodore Green cleared his throat. "I've recently talked with some worried members of our community about your–um–flying lessons. This is a highly unusual situation. One that in the entire history of this community we've never encountered."

He smoothed the crease of his trousers between his thumb and forefinger. "I'll have to admit I find it difficult to believe, but one person said she'd witnessed someone flying. If this is true, it must not continue."

Lillian pressed her fingertips together in her lap. "Why not? What harm can it do?"

"You're not denying it?"

"Of course not." She drew in a breath and huffed it back out. "Theodore Green, what is the matter with you? You know I'd never intentionally do anything harmful. Surely you know me that well. We were neighbors. I've known you and Agnes for years." But the image of that last town meeting when he had criticized Michael and scarcely looked at her flickered in her mind.

Theodore Green stood and paced about her living room, staring down at her. "Lillian, you're wrong, just as wrong as you can be. I don't know you at all. And this flying, if it is true, is outrageous. What if everyone started flying? The air would be chaos! People bumping into each other. Falling on the tops of our heads. Crashing onto the streets. Traffic jams. Broken legs, arms. It would never do if all of our solid, respectable citizens started flying." He fixed his gaze on Lillian, then sat back down on the sofa.

Harp notes rang from inside her handbag which she'd set on the floor beside her easy chair. Without looking, she reached over the arm of the chair, groped inside the handbag for her cell phone and pushed off the ringer

"I'm sorry this has been so upsetting," Lillian said. "It's all so sudden for you, so different. How about coming to one of our lessons? Maybe you'd feel differently if you saw us fly. We've been meeting—

or...." She glanced around her living room. "Or I could give you a small demonstration now?"

Theodore's face turned pale as if he'd suddenly stumbled over a corpse. Shaking his head, he scooted to the edge of the sofa. He was breathing rapidly. "No. You must stop this activity. At once. You do understand that?"

"But it's so wonderful. If you'd ever fly just once...."

Theodore Green's face turned red. His body trembled. He jabbed his forefinger at her. "Does that mean you're not going to cooperate?"

Lillian shook her head. "You haven't even let me explain—"

"No. Stop." Theodore Green stood and clenched his fingers into a fist. "I don't have time to talk nonsense. I'm taking this to the Town Council. Our next meeting is on Tuesday two weeks from yesterday. And it would be a good idea for you to be present. 7:30 at the Town Hall." He walked to the door, yanked it open and rushed outside.

Lillian closed the door and leaned against it. Now what?

She picked up her handbag from beside the chair. As she dug out her phone, it vibrated against her fingers. She looked at it. A second call from a number she didn't recognize. Whoever it was didn't leave a message. She deleted the calls, laid her phone on the coffee table, hung up her coat and scarf in the closet and carried her handbag back to her bedroom.

Chapter 17
Sally Runs Away

Lillian ate a bowl of chili and half an apple while sitting at her kitchen table. Then she walked back into the living room, settled down in the flowered easy chair with a fuzzy blanket wrapped around her and called the Wilsons. George Wilson answered. She told him about her visit with Theodore Green.

"We've been gone all day," George said. "We found a note from him stuck in our door, asking us to call him. I planned to call in the morning. We wondered what that was all about. Well, we'll phone him all right. And we'll be at that meeting too. Can we take you with us?"

"Thanks. I'd appreciate it. And I've decided to cancel our lesson Saturday. I plan to write a paper about flying to present at the council meeting. Maybe it will help clear up any misunderstandings. Also, I've already promised to meet a friend for lunch on

Saturday. I really need all the time I can find to spend writing that paper."

Next, she called Robby to tell him that the flying class wouldn't be meeting on Saturday.

"It's all my fault," Robby said. "I didn't mean to get everyone in trouble. But Mr. Green made me tell him everyone's names. He said he didn't want to have to use force."

Lillian gripped her cell phone. "He said that?"

"Yes."

"Robby, listen to me. First of all, you didn't do anything wrong. But Mr. Green did. He shouldn't have threatened you. And try not to worry. I'm planning to go to that meeting and give a paper about flying, plus offer to answer any questions anyone has about it."

The door buzzer sounded as she ended the call.

"Who's there?" she called walking to the door.

"Police. This is the police."

"Police?" Scarcely breathing, Lillian pulled open the door. "What's wrong?"

A uniformed police officer stood in the doorway. His silvery badge reflected the light from her table lamps. He straightened his shoulders as he looked into her eyes. "Are you Lillian Brown?"

"Yes."

"Do you know a little girl, Sally Jones?"

"Yes. Of course."

"Well, mam, she's missing. Her mother said maybe you knew something. Mrs. Jones said she tried to call you but never could reach you."

100

Lillian crossed her arms and hugged herself. "Well, Sally's not here. I doubt she even knows where I live. But come inside so I can close the door."

She stepped aside as the police officer walked past her into the living room. "What happened? How long has she been missing?"

"Not really sure, mam. Probably about three hours. Mrs. Jones said she was already upset because her father didn't want her to fly. Then when Mr. Green went over there, asking questions and saying he was going to put a stop to flying, she became hysterical. Mrs. Jones said she kept saying it wasn't fair."

"She said she'd talked with Sally and thought she'd calmed down. But when she went to her room to call her for dinner, her bedroom window was open and she was gone. Mrs. Jones said she and Mr. Jones had already checked with the neighbors."

"What about Robby Fulton and his father, and George and Grace Wilson? They're the others in the class."

"Someone's already checking with them."

Lillian stared into the officer's eyes. "Maybe she headed toward the meadow. That's where we hold the lessons. Or the school. One time she talked about the woods behind her school."

"Someone's checking out the meadow. But that's pretty far. I think someone already checked out the school."

Lillian ran the fingers of both hands up through her hair. "Where else could she have gone? Where?

Flying is so harmless. I never expected something like this to happen."

The police officer stared at Lillian. He turned his hat in his hands. "This is real? This flying? Like up in the air?"

Lillian nodded. "But now isn't the time to explain. I'm going to get my car and go over to the Jones's house."

"The police officer plunked his cap back on his head as he walked out the door. "A six-year-old shouldn't be out alone this time of night."

"I know, and it's also freezing cold." After grabbing her jacket and locking the door, Lillian picked her way across the icy walkway, down the steps into the parking lot, and got into her car. Where would Sally have gone? She could be anywhere.

Taking backstreets, Lillian drove the several blocks to the Jones's neighborhood. Small ranch houses with covered up barbeque grills in the back yards and bicycles and basketball hoops in the driveways lined both sides of the road. It was the kind of neighborhood where everyone knew everyone else, where neighbors looked out for and took care of each other.

Lillian's old neighborhood before her divorce had been that kind of neighborhood. Could she be happy there again if that ever became possible? Ridiculous even to consider. It would never happen.

When she reached the Jones's house, a light was on over the front door. The garage door was up and it was empty inside. Lillian drove beside the curb and switched off the ignition.

As she walked up the walkway, the front door of the house flew open and Marty rushed outside onto the porch. "Lillian? For a moment I thought you were Harry! Robby found her. She's at Robby's house. Harry's gone to get her. Come on inside and I'll tell you."

Lillian followed Marty into the living room. A faded rose-flowered sofa and matching green and yellow chairs were grouped around a beige area rug. In front of the sofa, a coffee table was covered with magazines, soda cans, paper towels and cheese and peanut butter cracker wrappers. Stacks of papers and a laundry basket of unfolded clothes sat on the floor beside the sofa. Lillian unzipped her jacket and pulled off her cap. She sat in one of the green chairs and Marty sat on the end of the sofa nearest her.

Lillian leaned toward Marty. "Is Sally all right? What happened?"

Marty looked down. She twisted the hem of her shirt. "Like I said, Robby found her. His dad called to let us know. I answered the phone. Harry was down at the police station. He was supposed to have stayed here. When we called the police they came here first. They told us to stay here in case anyone called. It was awful. Harry blamed himself for yelling at her. He said if anything had happened to her he would never forgive himself. He paced around the house like a caged animal. Finally, he said he couldn't stand just

103

sitting here. That's when he went down to the police station.

"I called him at the police station after Robby's dad called. He said it would be quicker if he went straight to the Fultons instead of coming by here and picking me up first." Marty's eyes watered, and she blotted them on her shirt sleeve. "Mr. Fulton said she was sleeping on their sofa, but she was all right." She stood up. "Excuse me, I'm going to go get a tissue."

Lillian nodded. "Thank goodness she's safe."

As Marty left the room, Lillian looked at her watch. Ten fifteen and she had to go to work in the morning.

A few moments later, Marty walked back into the room.

Several tissues fluttered from her hand. Her eyes and nose were red.

Lillian smiled. "Would you like for me to wait with you until Harry and Sally get here?"

"Oh, would you? Please."

Chapter 18
Lillian Waits with Marty

It was close to midnight when Harry carried Sally through the front doorway. Her head lay against his shoulder. "Shhh," he said as Marty rushed toward him.

Lillian stood at the entrance to the living room and watched. Harry was medium tall, thin and wiry. His dark, unkempt hair drooped over his forehead onto his glasses. Sally roused, lifting her head and blinking. She was wrapped in a blanket.

Sobbing, Marty, threw her arms around Sally. "Baby, baby, I'm so glad you're home."

Sally yawned. "Daddy isn't mad anymore."

"No," Harry said, his voice almost a whisper.

Sally yawned again. "I want to fly."

Harry glanced at Marty then looked back at Sally. "We'll talk about that in the morning. Right now it's bed time." He headed down the hall. Marty followed a few steps then stopped and looked back at Lillian. "I won't be long."

"Don't rush," Lillian said. "If you need to stay longer than I can wait, I'll let myself out." She walked back into the living room. Yawning, she sat in the same green chair.

Ten minutes later, she stood and slipped on her coat. She was lining up the zipper ends when Marty reappeared. "Harry's going to sit with her a little longer. But he said he wants to meet you if you can wait. He said he had an interesting talk with Robby's dad. That's why he was so late getting home."

Lillian stifled a yawn, causing her eyes to tear slightly. "All right. I'd like to meet him too."

Marty stared down at her hands which she'd clasped together in her lap. "Lillian, we were both so scared," she said softly. "He kept saying he never should've let her go with me to the lessons. He said that was all we ever talked about anymore."

Her eyes filled with tears. "We've been working so hard to get our landscaping business going. I don't want it to fail. We're not making enough to hire someone to do my job. We're barely getting by as it is. But I'm so unhappy the way things are now."

Lillian nodded.

"Harry said if I left we'd probably have to sell our business. I'd hate to do that. He loves working with plants more than anything."

Lillian frowned and shook her head slightly. "I don't like the idea of giving up your business either.

106

Especially without a lot of thought, since you both seem to have put so much of yourselves in it."

"I know," Marty said. "I kind of enjoy keeping the books. I've always liked working with numbers, but sometimes I get lonely working out of our home. Hardly ever seeing anyone. I love our flying lessons. I really enjoy being with you and the Wilsons and Robby."

Lillian and Marty looked up as Harry walked into the room. He stepped in front of Lillian and smiled. "I'm Harry and you must be Lillian Brown. Thanks for sticking around."

Lillian smiled. "You're welcome. I wanted to meet you. I'm sorry the flying lessons have created problems for your family."

Harry nodded. "That's something I want to talk with you about"

He sat on the sofa beside Marty. He took her hand and looked at Lillian.

"I heard you and Marty talking right before I came in—about us selling the business. Nothing's certain. Marty and I need to talk about several things. Did she tell you where they found Sally?"

Lillian shook her head.

Harry dropped Marty's hand and ran his fingers through his hair. "She was hiding in Robby's van." He looked into the distance and swallowed. When he spoke, his voice was low. "It seems she was planning to hide in the woods behind the school. But when she got to the school Robby was there playing basketball with some of his friends on the playground." He paused and cleared his throat.

"She decided to hide in his van until it was safe to sneak in the woods. There was a sleeping bag, tent and some other camping stuff in the van, and she hid under that. She told Robby she fell asleep.

"Robby said it was getting dark when they stopped playing basketball. He said he never looked in the back of his van, just got in and drove home. He said Sally told him she woke up but didn't know what to do and stayed hidden. When Robby got home, he said he parked in the drive and went inside the house. Later, when Marty called and the police came asking about her, he said he told them he had no idea where she was. He said it was only after he started driving around looking for her and heard her crying that he found her under all the camping stuff."

"He should have brought her here instead of taking her to his house," Marty said.

Harry ran his hands through his hair several times. "Robby told his dad she was crying, and she kept begging him not to take her back home. Mr. Fulton, of course, said they had to call us and let us know she was all right."

"Oh, Harry." Marty's eyes filled with tears. "She was that unhappy."

Harry's face turned red. "Yes," he said, his voice choked. "Mr. Fulton talked some about the flying. He said it's been good for Robby. He said if I wanted, he'd be glad to discuss it with me some more."

Lillian drew her lower lip in between her front teeth and bit down lightly.

Marty's eyes grew round. "Are you going to? Talk to him again?"

"I said I'd think about it. Of course, if it gets outlawed it won't be an issue." He looked at Lillian. "I guess you'll be going to that council meeting?"

"Yes, Theodore Green asked me to be present."

Harry looked at Marty. "Maybe we should go too?"

"Oh, Harry!"

"Thank you," Lillian said. "And Marty, I decided to cancel our lesson on Saturday. I've already told the others. I need the time to write a paper about flying and its benefits to present to the town council."

Chapter 19
Problems at Work

When Lillian finally climbed into bed, every muscle in her body ached. She lay flat on her back, and pressed the back of her head into the pillows. She pulled the sheet and blanket up to her chin, then stretched her arms and legs out straight. She wiggled her toes. At least Marty and her family and Robby and his father seemed calmer. But their situations were far from stable. She felt as depleted as a rag doll missing half its stuffing. How could so many problems have arisen just because she taught a few people how to fly?

The next morning at work, she had barely hung up her coat and scarf and cap when Sylvia Jeffers called. "I hate calling you at work, but— what's this rumor going around that you're teaching flying lessons and the town council's having a meeting about it?"

"Oh, Sylvia." Lillian looked out the window at the people rushing about on the sidewalk below. "I was

111

planning to tell you all about it Saturday at lunch. It's way too complicated to go into now."

"You mean it's true?"

"Well…yes, but. Sylvia, please, try to understand."

"Oh, all right. I guess I can wait another day. See you Saturday."

After hanging up, Lillian walked out into the reception room. Sherry sat at her desk, stirring powdered creamer into her coffee mug while she chatted with two of the other counselors. All three grinned and rolled their eyes at each other. Lillian forced a smile. She asked Sherry please not to put through any personal calls.

Sherry shrugged and glanced at the other counselors. "All right."

Midmorning there was a knock on Lillian's office door.

"Come in." She closed the file she'd been writing in. She looked up as Will Hawkins walked through the doorway. He waved a yellow slip of paper as if it was a tiny flag. His face was red, and he had loosened the knot of his tie. The ends of the tie fell off to one side of his shirt. His black hair was mussed all over as if wind had blown through it causing it to stand out on end. When he spoke his voice trembled. "Lillian, …would...you...please...come...to my…office?"

"Certainly." Lillian shoved the file in her bottom desk drawer and closed it. She stood and sauntered behind him across the reception room to his office. On the way, she smiled and held out the palms of her hands toward Sherry trying to imply that she hadn't a clue what this was about.

Once inside Will Hawkins's office, he pointed at the chair in front of his desk. "Have a seat." He then shut the door and sat down behind his desk. He ran a finger around the inside of his collar.

He wiped his forehead with a white handkerchief that had been folded and refolded into a small, even square and leaned across his desk. "Will you please tell me what is going on?" He shook the yellow slip of paper at her. "I just had a call from the newspaper...that you're...you're…giving flying lessons."

Lillian's cheeks burned. She willed herself to look directly into his eyes, which right now were gazing into hers with a deep grey-green steely quality. "It's kind of hard to explain," she said and swallowed. "But it's true, and there's apparently been some opposition."

Will Hawkins' face turned redder. "You mean you're not denying it."

Lillian shook her head. "No." If only she could stand up, walk out and fly away. If only she could fly wherever she wanted to fly, whenever she wanted to fly, even forever if she chose.

"This is incredible. I can't believe what I'm hearing you say. You've always been dependable, stable, conscientious— and now you sit there and tell me you're teaching flying lessons?"
"Yes."

"I think you'd better take a few days off and get some rest." He stared over her head into space.

"Does this mean I might get fired?"

Will Hawkins wiped his face again. "What I said was 'take some time off.' Why didn't you come to me about this first? You know there's a policy about not conducting private counseling sessions."

"But this isn't that. It's flying lessons."

"I know that," he exploded. "But you still should've come to me about it. Then this whole issue might have been avoided."

Lillian pressed her fingertips together tightly. "Then you don't believe I really can—"

"I don't know what to believe. You seem sane and rational— but flying? Please tell me this is some kind of a joke. Please."

Lillian stared into his eyes, straightening her back and throwing back her shoulders. "But it isn't."

For a long time, Will Hawkins gazed at her without speaking. The only sounds were the fluorescent lights humming overhead, and from out in the reception room, the muffled laughter of Sherry and one of the counselors.

Finally, Will Hawkins shook his head and pointed at the door. "All right. You can go now."

Lillian walked back to her office, keeping her eyes straight ahead. She cleared the papers off her desk and locked it. Everything, her entire life was in chaos, a stupendous, colossal mess. Scarcely aware of what she was doing, she lifted her coat and knit cap off the coatrack and slipped them on. Her thoughts collided inside her head. Whatever was she going to do now? When she walked out the counseling office door, Sherry's "Goodbye" came from miles away.

Chapter 20
Robby Has a Plan

The next day, an announcement appeared in the local section of the newspaper stating that the main issue to be discussed at the council meeting, one week from Tuesday, was whether or not flying and flying lessons should be permitted in Green Valley. The public was encouraged to attend.

On the editorial page, a cartoon showed the council members bumping into each other as they flew high in the sky. Lillian stood below watching, a quizzical expression on her face. A caption underneath read, "Will the flying school crash land?"

Lillian's cell phone rang several times with journalists calling from the newspaper and local TV station. Finally, she tapped the "Do Not Disturb" app on her phone and put the phone face down on her coffee table. Too much. She didn't want to talk about it. She needed a break. The rest of the day she worked on her flying paper.

That evening, when she walked into the kitchen to prepare dinner and switched on the TV, an announcer was saying, "...and a rumor is making the local news tonight. Lillian Brown, a family counselor, reportedly, has been giving flying lessons. Some worried members of the community are so upset about possible wide-spread effects that ...." A photograph of Lillian flashed on the screen. In the picture, her hair was shoulder-length and turned under on the ends. She had looked a lot like Karen at that age. Where had they gotten that picture? It was at least fifteen years old.

She turned the TV off, and after eating and cleaning up the kitchen, played her piano for an hour and went to bed.

Promptly at 6:00 a.m. Saturday morning, Lillian got out of bed and went straight to her computer.

She was still in her pajamas and fleece bathrobe two hours later when she took a break and walked outside to get the morning newspaper. Running up the steps from the parking lot toward her were Robby and Sally.

Lillian stared at them. "Robby? Sally? What're you two doing here?"

Robby scooped up the paper and handed it to her. "We've got a great idea. And the Joneses and Wilsons agree."

"We're going to put on a show," Sally said.

"A show?" Lillian said. "What kind?"

118

"A flying demonstration," Robby said. "I've already talked to Dad, and he said he'd help Mrs. Jones with the posters."

"The posters are for the show. Next Saturday." Sally grinned at Robby.

Robby nodded. "I thought if we put on a demonstration, everyone would see how great flying is. Then the council members will vote to approve it."

"Mommy said she'd call all the neighbors and ask them to be on a committee," Sally said. "We're going to have refreshments."

"We kept trying to call you," Robby said, "All we need is for you to say all right,"

Lillian stared at Robby and Sally. She never took her phone off "Do Not Disturb." Never even thought about it.

Would a demonstration help? Make any real difference? Anything was possible. "But we'd have to practice and put together a really special routine."

"Yeah, right," Robby said. "Like this afternoon. It's the only time everyone can get together. Can you figure out something that quick?"

"Probably." This might be better than a paper anyway. But Sylvia? She'd promised to meet her at 1:00 for lunch. She couldn't cancel that. Their friendship was already fragile. But if she and her students rehearsed, it would have to be early before it got too cold and dark. Could she do both? Surely Sylvia wouldn't mind moving their lunch appointment back an hour to 12:00.

"All right," Lillian said. "Let's try it."

"Yeah," said Sally, clapping her hands and jumping up and down.

Robby grinned at Lillian. "Great. You want me to call the others?" He paused. "Is it true you might get fired because of all this?"

Lillian shook her head. "Of course not. You must have heard a rumor." But her breath caught. Will Hawkins hadn't said how long to take off, but he sure hadn't meant forever. Soon she'd have to go back.

Sally grabbed Lillian's arm. "Guess what? We found out who started all the trouble. Mrs. Tilson and Mrs. Snell."

Robby glared. "The Snells live next door to us. Mrs. Snell saw me fly across the backyard that one time. She told her friend, Mrs. Tilson."

Sally shook Robby's arm and looked up at Lillian. "We found out because Mrs. Wilson told Mommy she saw Mrs. Tilson in the elevator at the retirement home. Mrs. Tilson bragged and said she was the one who called Mr. Green. She said flying could lead to bad things."

Lillian shook her head. "She decided it was bad even though she knows nothing about it except what her friend told her?"

Sally nodded. "Mrs. Wilson told Mommy that she told Mrs. Tilson she ought to try it, that she might see things differently."

Lillian smiled. "Maybe one day she will." Maddening as it was, she felt a little sorry for Evie and

120

Mrs. Snell. They had to be very frightened, deep inside, to refuse even to consider anything new and different.

After several phone calls back and forth, everyone agreed to meet at the meadow that afternoon at 2:15.

Chapter 21
Lillian Meets Sylvia for Lunch

At five minutes before twelve Lillian stepped between the double glass doors into COUSIN SOPHIE'S. Already, people waiting to be seated filled the area near the cashier's counter. Lillian looked around the restaurant, hoping Sylvia was already there. But there was no sign of her.

After telling the hostess she wanted a table for two, Lillian positioned herself with her back to the counter so she could watch the entrance. She glanced over her shoulder at the overhead clock behind the counter. 11:58. Why hadn't she thought to call in a reservation?

At 11:59, Sylvia walked through the restaurant doors. Lillian waved at her.

"Hi," Sylvia said rushing to her. "I was almost late. I couldn't find a parking place. I had to go all the way up to .... Never mind. I can't wait to talk and get caught up. I've got a ton of questions."

Lillian ran her tongue across the inside of her lower lip. "Me too. I can't wait to talk either." She stared around them at the clumps of people standing beside or sitting on a vinyl sofa and two matching chairs. "I just wish I'd made a reservation."

Sylvia shrugged. "No problem. I've got the whole afternoon free." Her eyes narrowed. "Or is there a problem?"

Lillian glanced at the clock. She cleared her throat. "Not really. I'm not in a rush, but I—uh—do kind of have to leave by 1:15."

Sylvia frowned. "Why didn't you tell me? We could've picked another day."

"I didn't want to reschedule. It's already been too long since we've gotten together. It's just that this other thing came up, and I couldn't—" The couple closest to Lillian had stopped talking and was obviously listening. Lillian glared at them until they moved away. "I didn't want you to think I didn't want...." she continued. "I mean I'd already...."

Sylvia shrugged out of her heavy quilted parka and held it in front of her. "You know, sometimes you annoy me. Sometimes I wonder how well I know you anymore."

Lillian lowered her voice. "I know. I'm sorry. I mean you're my best friend, and I'm never available. If it was the other way around, I'd be annoyed too."

She glanced at the clock. "I do wish they'd hurry and seat us though. I hate people listening in."

Sylvia shifted the coat about in her arms and drew her lips into a line.

Gradually the reception area cleared, and at last the hostess headed toward them clutching two outsized, red, vinyl-covered menus against her chest. She smiled. "If you'll come with me, please, I have a table ready now."

After the waiter had taken their orders, Lillian looked across the table at Sylvia. "You're upset."

Sylvia's lips curved into a smile, but the expression in her eyes was blank. She shook her head slightly. "Not really. But I do feel bad you felt obligated to see me."

"No, it's not that. I don't feel obligated. Not at all. It's just that, for a variety of reasons that I can't go into now, I haven't found a big enough block of time to get with you to explain what's been going on in my life. There's no way you could possibly understand without me telling you."

Sylvia's eyes grew red and watery. "No. I guess you're right. I don't understand."

Lillian glanced at her watch. 12:40. "Sylvia, please, listen to me because I'll have to be brief." She paused while the waiter set their plates in front of them and refilled their water glasses.

She continued. "It was a really big struggle, but I finally taught myself how to fly."

Sylvia's eyes opened wide. She drew in her cheeks and narrowed her eyes as she began poking her fork around in her salad.

"It's true," Lillian said. "I flew around in my apartment at first, but then I needed more space, and ...well, flying was so wonderful, I decided to teach it."

Sylvia cut a lettuce leaf in half with the side of her fork. She shook her head. "Why are you talking nonsense like this?" Her lower lip trembled. "I thought we were friends."

"We are friends." Lillian looked at her watch. Almost one. They'd hardly touched their food. "I know what, I should've thought of this sooner. Let's hurry and eat. Then you can come with me to the meadow and watch us fly.

"We're going to practice for a demonstration we're going to put on for the town. That's why I have to leave early. To practice for that. You said you had the afternoon free. We can talk on the way there and back. If you can see us fly, that's far better than me trying to explain."

Sylvia's eyes widened. She smiled a tight half-smile. "I didn't mean I had the afternoon free literally. Maybe some other time."

The remainder of their meal they ate in silence. Then they picked up their separate bills and walked single file to the cashier.

Chapter 22
Robby Gets Bruised

Lillian arrived at the meadow at 2:05. The Wilsons were jumping up and down and swinging their arms to warm up. Mrs. Wilson dashed toward her. "Lillian, I just know as soon as everyone sees us, they can't help but love what we're doing."

"Sure hope so," Mr. Wilson said, stepping beside Mrs. Wilson. "Because we're really enjoying life again." He held up a camera. "Look what I dug out of the closet. I've been taking pictures of Mrs. Wilson's bluegrass group. Now I want to take some of us flying. I might sign up for a photography course at the community college."

"That sounds great." Lillian forced her voice to sound enthusiastic. She really was glad for George Wilson. But what about Sylvia? Sylvia was still upset when they left the restaurant. Robby's van rattled to a stop, followed by Marty and Sally's car.

Robby limped slightly as he walked toward Lillian and the Wilson's. He was wearing dark glasses. A purplish bruise spread across one cheek and up under one lens of his sunglasses. Both of his lips were swollen.

"Robby," Lillian said. "What happened to you?"

Robby shrugged. "Nothing. I tripped and fell."

Sally shook her head. "Daddy said your daddy said you got in a fight at school."

Everyone stared at Robby.

Lillian waved both arms. "Listen folks, we need to start practicing our routine. The demonstration is exactly one week from today. Right now is our only time to practice."

She let the others walk ahead and stepped beside Robby. "You look like you're hurting. If you want, you can skip the practice. I can work with you later in the week. You're so advanced you won't need much practice"

Robby shook his head. "I'm good. The demonstration was my idea. Oh, I helped Sally and Mrs. Jones make a bunch of posters. Dad said he'd put one up in his office."

"That's great."

"Mrs. Jones said she was bringing one for you."

"Thanks. I'd already planned to stop by the office sometime next week. I'll ask if I can put it up in the reception room."

In the center of the meadow, the students spread into a large semicircle in front of Lillian.

But before Lillian could speak, Mrs. Wilson waved both arms. She broke away from the others and ran beside Lillian. "I've got an announcement to make. I didn't want to forget. First, George and I want all of you to come eat with us next Friday evening. And second, I'm making presents for each of you."

Sally jumped up and down. "What are they?"

"That's a surprise. I'll give them out Friday."

Chapter 23

Karen Confronts Lillian

When Lillian returned home, she found a folded note stuck in her door. She opened the note. "Call me at once, Karen."

Now what? Lillian unlocked the door and walked inside. She punched in Karen's number and listened to ringing on the other end.

"Mother!" Karen's voice exploded in Lillian's ears. "The whole town's talking about you! I'm coming over."

"Karen. Calm down. I admit things have gotten a little out of hand. But, never mind. Come on over."

Twenty minutes later, a car door slammed outside in the parking lot. A moment later the buzzer on Lillian's door sounded. Lillian barely had opened the door when Karen brushed past her inside.

Her face was pale. "Mother, what is going on? It's embarrassing. Do you realize how old you are?"

Lillian reached toward her. "I keep trying to explain, but you never will listen."

"But it's not true. No one can really fly. You can't imagine what everyone's saying?"

Lillian crisscrossed her arms in front of her chest. "No, and please don't tell me."

Karen glared, pursing her lips. "Mom, I'm worried about how this will affect my job. That Mr. Bryant will wonder if—if I might be—like you. Her face scrunched up as if she were about to cry.

Lillian raked her fingers through her hair. "Honey, you're my only child, and I love you dearly. I wouldn't hurt you for anything. Do you really think Mr. Bryant would think badly of you just because of something your mother did?"

"Mother, please. All you'd have to do is call the paper and say this is a joke. Then, hopefully, things will quiet down in a few days, and life will go on as usual."

"But it's not a joke, and life can be better than usual. Anyway, we're giving a flying demonstration on the town green next Saturday. I hope you'll come. You might see things differently."

Tears welled up in Karen's eyes. "No. I'd feel too humiliated. I hope they vote against you."

Chapter 24

Dinner at the Wilsons'

By Monday morning, posters announcing the flying demonstration had already appeared on telephone poles and in store windows. Marty's committee organized a drawing contest and talked a toy store into donating prizes. The committee also arranged to borrow long folding tables from a church for the refreshments. Without being asked, a hardware store decided to sell helium-filled balloons.

Harry Jones and Charles Fulton met for lunch on two occasions and discussed the flying school. Charles told Harry that the lessons had helped Robby. During one of their conversations, Harry admitted that he'd worried that if Sally and Marty continued flying, he didn't know what else they might be able to do. He said he was afraid he might end up losing them. When later he told Marty what he'd said to Charles, she told him that she felt closer to him then than she ever had and would never leave him.

Harry was so relieved that he offered to be the announcer for the demonstration. He even made a banner, LILLIAN'S FLYING SCHOOL, out of an old sheet. Mr. Wilson agreed to help him hang it over the street that ran between the green and the town hall. Mrs. Wilson worked night and day on her presents. Lillian telephoned both Karen and Sylvia several times, but they never returned her calls.

At 6:00 on Friday evening, Lillian rode the elevator up to the sixth floor of the Green Valley Retirement Community building. She walked down the carpeted hallway to the Wilsons' door and pressed the buzzer. George Wilson welcomed her inside.

"Everyone's here," Robby called as he hurried to Lillian with his father close behind. His limp was gone and the bruises on his cheek had faded from purple to a yellowish green. The swelling had gone down in his lips.

Charles Fulton held out his hand. "Lillian, it's good seeing you again."

Lillian smiled. "I'm glad too."

Sally threw her arms around Lillian's waist. "Now we can get our presents."

"I can't wait," Lillian said, hugging her back.

Sally dashed back across the living room. "Ms. Wilson! Ms. Wilson! Ms. Lillian's here!"

After hanging Lillian's coat in the closet, George Wilson excused himself. "I need to go back out to the patio. The coals in the grill should be ready. Robby, you want to help put on the hamburgers?"

After Robby and George Wilson walked away, Charles smiled at Lillian. "Can I get you something to drink? A soda—coffee?"

"Mmm, a soda, thanks." Lillian observed him as he walked toward the kitchen. His shoulders slumped slightly. There was a worn place on one elbow of his grey sweater. It was tough being a single parent.

Mrs. Wilson bustled toward her. "Poor Robby. George and I have been so worried about him. We talked to his father about it. Of course we invited both him and Harry Jones to come tonight. I'm so excited about tomorrow, I can hardly stand it."

Lillian nodded. "I'm excited too, but I'm also nervous."

Mrs. Wilson patted her arm. "Now don't you worry. Everything's going to be just fine. We've rehearsed. Our routine is perfect. And on top of that clear weather is predicted for all day tomorrow." She glanced at Sally who was heading toward them. "Sally's about to have a fit to give out the gifts. I told her she had to help wrap them first because I ran out of time to do it myself." Mrs. Wilson intercepted Sally and they disappeared into the hall.

Lillian sat down on the sofa. Charles had stopped beside the dining table and was speaking to Marty and Harry who were setting a stack of plates and silverware on the table. She thought back to her conversation the past Saturday with Karen. What about Michael and his wife separating? What about him asking about her? What about all the years she'd hoped he'd come back? She'd lived alone a long time. Most of the time she'd been too busy to be lonely. What were her feelings about her ex now?

Robby and Mr. Wilson were out on the patio tending the hamburgers. Robby seemed subdued. He had participated fully when they practiced their routine on Saturday. After the practice he had talked about the fight as they walked back to their cars. He had seemed pretty much all right. She breathed in the burnt wood scent of the charcoal smoke. Such a short time ago, all but the Wilsons had been complete strangers. Now they were almost like family.

Charles returned and handed her a canned soda. He set a bowl of potato chips on the coffee table then sat beside her. "Again, thanks for helping with Robby. Except for a little scuffle at school, he's doing fairly well. He seems to really enjoy the lessons."

Lillian smiled. "Thank you for telling me. Robby's an important member of our group." She reached for a potato chip. "But judging by how he looked last Saturday that hardly seemed like just 'a little scuffle.'"

Charles frowned then half smiled. "You'd make a good lawyer. Did he tell you what happened?"

Lillian nodded. "We talked about it some."

Charles set his plate on the coffee table. "Did he tell you the kid he got in a fight with was Theodore Green's son? The principal said Green and several other kids were mocking him during lunch period. Chirping and flapping their arms like wings. He told me that Robby tore into Green's son, breaking his glasses. Then the other kids piled on Robby."

Lillian's breath caught. Robby hadn't told her the part about being ganged up on. Or about breaking anyone's glasses. "Anyway, I'm glad you came with him tonight. The demonstration tomorrow is big for him. It's big for all of us. He needs your support. Did you know the idea for doing it was his idea?"

Charles shook his head. When he spoke again his voice was low. "He's like his mother was in some ways—creative, kind of a rebel." He paused. "Had you heard I'm a widower?"

"Yes."

"He and his mother were close. He took it hard when she died." He set his soda on his knee and ran his finger down the side of the can. Water droplets ran off the can and soaked into his pant leg. "Up until then, he'd been a good student. After she died, he started hanging out with some older kids who were into drinking, drugs, etcetera. He argued with his teachers, stopped doing his homework. He hardly said a civil word. I took him for counseling, but he refused to talk."

Lillian glanced across the room at the balcony. Robby and Mr. Wilson were still bent over the hamburgers. She looked back at Charles. "You're a lawyer. I'm sure you're as aware as I am that people handle grief in different ways. Sometimes a person

137

may take out some of their feelings on themselves or others." She paused. "Sometimes it's just too painful to admit who they're really angry with."

Charles looked into the distance for several moments. "Like maybe his mother?"

Lillian nodded.

"You may be right. He was definitely angry. It's been a year and an half and I still get angry at times. It was totally her fault for driving fast on that icy road. I'd warned her a dozen times." He paused. "Anyway, things are better now with Robby."

"I'm glad. My daughter and I have had our share of conflicts." Between sips of soda, she told him a little about herself and Karen.

After she finished, Charles pulled off his glasses and wiped them on the front of his shirt. "We seem to have a few things in common. Maybe we can get together again sometime and talk more?"

They looked up as Mrs. Wilson and Sally hurried back into the living room. Sally carried a stack of gift-wrapped boxes in her arms.

Chapter 25

George Wilson's Story

"Everyone, come find a seat," Mrs. Wilson called out. "We're ready to hand out the gifts." As she read their names, Sally handed out the brightly wrapped boxes.

Mrs. Wilson smiled at Charles and Harry. "I'm sorry I don't have anything for you, but I made these only for the first flying students."

Lillian waited until all the gifts had been handed out before unwrapping hers. Slowly lifting the lid off the box, she spread apart the white tissue wrap and took out a red felt vest with LILLIAN'S FLYING SCHOOL appliquéd in large black letters across the back.

Sally unwrapped an identical vest of blue felt. Marty's was purple, Robby's green, Mr. Wilson's orange and Mrs. Wilson's a shocking pink.

Harry grinned. "No matter how high you fly, with those bright colors we won't have any trouble seeing you."

Mrs. Wilson beamed. "I know. I wanted them to be alike *and* different."

"What a great idea," Marty said. "If the council passes flying, you could go into business making vests."

Mrs. Wilson shook her head. "I've already started a writing project that matters more, but I don't want to talk about it until after Tuesday night."

Lillian's heart fluttered, making it hard for her to breathe for a moment. How would the council vote? She couldn't bear having to stop flying and to give up teaching.

Marty slipped on her purple vest and stood up. "I think we should have a fashion show!" At once Sally put on her blue vest and began buttoning it.

Only Robby remained sitting on the floor. He stared at the green vest draped across his knees.

Mrs. Wilson walked to him and leaned down. "What's wrong? Don't you like it?"

Robby looked up at her. "No. It's not that. It's just...I mean...."

Mr. Wilson stepped beside Mrs. Wilson. He touched her shoulder and looked at Robby. He lowered himself onto the floor beside him. "Does it have anything to do with the fact that none of your friends will be wearing a vest with LILLIAN'S FLYING SCHOOL written on the back?"

140

Robby's face turned red. He laid his vest back in the box and set the box on the floor. He untied the laces on his sneakers. He tied the laces again, carefully looping the end of one lace over the other.

His father leaned over the arm of the sofa and placed his hand on Robby's shoulder. "Get on up there with the others. I just heard how this whole demonstration was your idea."

Lillian shook her head. "It's all right. He doesn't...."

"Ooh, my goodness," Mrs. Wilson said. "Robby, don't give the vest another thought. You certainly don't have to wear it." She looked around at the others. "Anyway, let's skip the fashion show. I'm sure the hamburgers are ready."

Later, after everyone had filled their plates, settled back down and were laughing and talking to each other, Mr. Wilson looked down at Robby who was sitting on the floor beside his chair. Robby was staring at his plate while he ate. "Hey there, Robby, you're mighty quiet. Still feeling bad?"

Robby shrugged and swallowed. "A little. I feel bad about Mrs. Wilson and all the work she did. Also, it's the kids at school. Some of them keep laughing and flapping their elbows every time I walk by."

Mr. Wilson nodded. "Forget about the vest. Mrs. Wilson understands." He looked into the distance a moment.

"Robby, you've reminded me of a time when I was around your age. I'd like to tell you about it."

Robby nodded.

"There was something I very much wanted to do. But I was scared about what would happen if I did."

Robby gazed at him.

Mr. Wilson set his plate on the small table beside his chair.

"Before that, let me go back a little. I grew up on a farm. Sometimes when my older brother was mowing the pasture, he let me sit behind him on the tractor seat. But one time soon after my ninth birthday, there had been a lot of rain and the grass was high. My brother didn't see this certain ditch and one of the tractor wheels slipped in it. The tractor turned over and I fell off the seat and rolled under some of the mower blades.

"I was fortunate because I had good doctors, and after a long stay in the hospital ended up with only a lot of scars. But I was convinced that as a result of the scars, I was a freak. After that I always wore long-sleeved shirts that I buttoned up to my neck."

Slowly, he unbuttoned the top three buttons of his shirt. Wide white scars ran from behind his neck and across the lower part of his throat. "These scars and others go all across my upper arms, back and chest all the way to my waist." He paused and took a long breath.

"One thing I'd always enjoyed as a kid was swimming in the river that ran by our farm. I got to be a fairly good swimmer. When I entered high school, I wanted to try out for the swimming team. They didn't have synthetic fabrics back then. If I'd worn a heavy soggy wet shirt, I never could have competed with the other swimmers." He grinned. "Even if the coach would have allowed it."

Robby's gaze moved over the scars on Mr. Wilson's neck and throat.

Mr. Wilson half-smiled. "The first few times I swam, there were a lot of stares and whispers. Sometimes I would overhear comments in the halls or see someone point and snicker. But the members of the swim team got used to seeing my scars and didn't treat me any differently than they did anyone else. A couple of them even said they admired my courage. And at one of the meets, I met Mrs. Wilson who was a diver on an opposing team."

Mr. Wilson rebuttoned his shirt. "I was never a champion swimmer, but I've always been glad I tried out for that team."

The others gradually had stopped talking and were listening.

Mr. Wilson grinned at them. "One advantage of being seventy-nine is not having to worry so much about appearances."

Sally set down her plate and crawled beside Robby. "I'm not worried and I'm just six."

"And that's probably why," Mrs. Wilson said. "Most six-year-olds wouldn't think flying was weird. They'd be too busy just trying to fly."

Lillian looked into her students' faces. "I know one thing. No matter how the council votes, I feel very fortunate to have all of you for friends. Nothing can take away our friendship."

While they discussed where and what time to meet the next morning, Mr. Wilson passed around more hamburgers. Marty invited Lillian to eat breakfast with their family in the morning and go with them to the town green.

Later, after everyone had carried their empty plates and cups to the kitchen, thanked the Wilsons and hugged everyone goodbye, Charles took Lillian's coat out of the closet. He held it while she slipped her arms into the sleeves. "This has been one of the most interesting and unusual evenings I've ever experienced. I look forward to seeing you again tomorrow."

Lillian's cheeks grew warm. "Yes, yes, it has been, I mean, so do I. I mean.... It has been. Interesting." She rummaged in her pockets for her gloves, then dropped one of them on the floor.

Chapter 26
The Demonstration

The next morning Lillian woke up early. She pulled back the curtains from her bedroom window and looked outside. Sunlight streamed through the bare tree branches. A beautiful day! Perfect for flying. Her heart thudded against her ribs. The demonstration just had to go well. Her students flew well. Especially to be so new at it. But they'd only rehearsed once. And never in front of an audience. Stop doubting, she told herself. Imagine flying.

After pulling on fleece-lined leggings and a long-sleeved sweater, she put on her red felt vest. She pulled on wool socks, stepped into waterproof sneakers and put on her warmest insulated jacket. She gathered up her favorite red and white-striped knit scarf, cap and mittens and stood by the living room window to wait for Harry and Sally.

On the way to the Jones's house, Lillian sat in the front seat of the car next to Harry. Sally sat in back.

Harry glanced at Lillian. "Marty said you seemed a little anxious last night."

"I am. I guess I'm not very good at hiding things."

"Well, you haven't heard my speech! It's a masterpiece!"

Sally leaned forward against her seat belt. "What's a masterpiece?"

Harry grinned at her in the rearview mirror. "Something great, fantastic."

Lillian smiled. "Whatever are you going to say?"

"Nothing outrageous. But maybe it will convince a few skeptics to keep an open mind."

Lillian laughed and the muscles loosened across her chest and shoulders.

When they arrived at the Jones's house, Marty met them at the back door. She had pulled her dark hair back into a pony tail. Her face glowed. "Only two hours and we'll be flying above the town."

"I know," Lillian said, stepping inside. She slipped off her coat and scarf and straightened her red vest.

Marty grabbed her arm. "No matter what happens at that council meeting, flying is here to stay." Sally and Harry nodded.

"I agree," Lillian said. "In some future time flying will probably be commonplace. But I don't want to have to wait until some vague distant time; I want to fly now, I want to be able to teach anyone who's interested now."

After breakfast, while Sally and Marty finished dressing, Harry loaded the dishwasher. Lillian perched on a stool in the kitchen, talking to him.

Harry paused and looked at Lillian. "I kept thinking last night at the Wilson's how different Marty and Sally and the others in your class are from a lot of the people I know. Actually, I've thought a lot since the night Sally ran away."

His voice dropped. "If anything bad had happened to Sally, and Marty and I had split, I wouldn't have had anything left that mattered."

Lillian nodded.

Harry looked at her. "I don't understand it. Even though flying is probably more important to them than anything else, we're a lot closer now than before."

"That's because flying frees and opens out life," Lillian said softly. "It doesn't stifle and exclude."

Later, at the town green, Lillian and the Jones family walked among the crowds of people looking for Grace and George Wilson and Robby and his father. People in winter jackets and parkas wandered past tables of layered cakes and cookies. Children dashed by, clutching the strings of colorful, helium-filled balloons.

"Do you think they really can fly?" one person asked the person beside her.

"That's what they're claiming," the other person replied.

147

Through the crowd, the Wilsons and Robby and Charles appeared. Their knit caps were pulled down over their ears and their cheeks were red. They had zipped their jackets to their chins. They hurried toward Lillian and the Jones family. Lillian waved at them. She was relieved that Robby had come. Last night she hadn't been sure.

"Would you believe it?" Mrs. Wilson said. "We walked right by Evie Tilson, and she had the nerve to look the other way when I said 'Hello.' But I'm not going to give her another thought."

Mr. Wilson swung his arms back and forth. Each time he lifted his arms, the hem of his orange vest showed beneath his jacket. "I never felt more like flying. I just wish all my retired friends could see me today."

Across the park, Lillian spotted Will Hawkins. He was standing beside Sherry, their secretary, and two of the other family counselors. She waved and they waved back. At least they were smiling.

As she had suspected, Will Hawkins had refused to let her put up a poster when she stopped by the office. "Lillian, you know advertising posters are against agency policy." Then he'd looked at her in a professional evaluating sort of way and asked, "By the way, when do you think you'll feel up to coming back?' She replied that she'd never *not* felt "up to coming back."

But how might this demonstration and the outcome of the council meeting on Tuesday night affect her job long term? Though right now she could hardly bear the thought of returning. And she was years away from retirement. Her heart fluttered like the wings of a trapped bird.

Harry pointed toward a microphone on a metal pole in the middle of the green. "It's almost time. Why don't all of you stand over to the side of that? And good luck!"

Sally hugged Lillian around the waist. "I love you, Ms. Lillian."

"I love you too," Lillian said, hugging her back. "All of you," she added and embraced each student.

"We won't let you down," Robby said, unzipping his jacket. He smoothed down his green vest and grinned.

Lillian's eyes teared. "I know you won't." She raised her voice and looked at her students. "Listen everyone. This is important. Remember, you are really flying for yourselves and not for me or anyone else."

Lillian and her students spread out into a wide semicircle beside Harry while he adjusted the microphone. He lightly thumped the wire covering of the microphone a couple of times, causing it to boom. The green grew still and hushed.

People crowded the green, standing in several places, almost all the way back to the sidewalk. Some were still arriving.

Harry grinned. "Good morning, everyone. Welcome to the first public demonstration of LILLIAN'S FLYING SCHOOL!"

149

While he introduced the students and told a little about their backgrounds, Lillian looked through the crowd hoping to see Karen. More people had showed up than she'd expected. She recognized many of them, but there was not a sign of Karen.

Standing next to Sylvia and Ed Jeffers was her ex-husband. Her heart missed a beat. She hadn't actually seen Michael in several years, though she had, on a few occasions, talked with him on the phone concerning business matters. He was still just as tall and skinny, and he was wearing jeans and sneakers, his usual attire away from work. He had on the same faded tan parka he'd worn for years. Was he still working at that same computer company? Karen rarely talked about him, and Lillian didn't like to quiz her and risk sounding too interested.

She looked away so he wouldn't catch her staring. Their divorce had been civilized enough, but she'd been devastated that morning when, just after Karen had run out the door to catch the school bus, he announced that he no longer wanted to be married to her.

With the support of therapy, she'd resigned her volunteer tutoring job at Karen's school and applied for a full-time counseling position with Green Valley Human Resources. But, oh how she had missed Michael.

Off to one side, Theodore Green, was talking to several people. His body looked stiff, and he was shaking his head in an angry way.

150

Lillian focused her attention back onto Harry. He held the microphone with one hand and gestured with his other while he spoke.

"...and now," he was saying, "I want to tell you that this is maybe the best thing that ever happened to my family. At first, I objected. I didn't think it was possible to fly. Then when I saw Sally fly, I worried about what else she might be able to do. I worried about where she might go. I was afraid I might lose my family. Instead, flying has brought us closer. I plan to be first in line to sign up for Lillian's next class."

"But I've talked long enough. Now let's welcome Lillian Brown and her flying school students. Watch them with open minds. Then if you believe flying to be a worthwhile activity, tell your representatives on the council to vote 'yes' on Tuesday. Let's all of us give Lillian and her students our support, so Lillian can continue teaching and all of us can learn to fly."

After a light applause, the green grew quiet. The only sounds were the LILLIAN'S FLYING SCHOOL banner flapping above the street and church bells ringing in the distance.

Lillian and her students took off their parkas and jackets and dropped them onto the ground. They would warm up quickly once they started flying. Lillian straightened her vest and pulled her red and white stocking cap down over her ears. She knotted the matching scarf around her neck.

She stepped in front of her students and looked into each face. "Forget about all the people watching.

Fly because this is what you want to do more than anything else in the whole world! Fly the way you want to fly. And if you want to do variations on our routine, that's all right."

She stepped back in place. "All right! Are you ready?"

One at a time, first Lillian, then each student sucked in a deep breath and jumped.

Lillian zoomed toward the sky, cold winter air whizzing past her face and body, her vest only a red smear.

Above her, white clouds were piled high like gigantic dollops of frozen vanilla yogurt in the blue sky. Far below on the green, people, trees and traffic sounds faded into nothingness. If only she could go on like this forever.

Just under the biggest cloud, she leveled her body and waited for the others. Her students in their new vests were bright splashes of color. The sunlight reflecting off them made them appear lit from within.

Once they were all together, they flew into a tight "V" formation with Lillian in front. Then as they had practiced, they flew as fast as they could four times back and forth above the town green. From below, a big "Ohhhhh" rose up from the crowd.

"Don't pay any attention," called out Lillian. "Just fly."

The students flew into an enormous circle. Whooping, shouting and waving to each other, they rolled over and over in somersaults. They dropped, executing backward dives and unbelievable twists. They raced after each other playing flying tag. They flew into an air current and spiraled so high they were only tiny dots in the sky.

Finally, Lillian pointed toward the ground and they dived, aiming for the small, cleared space beside Harry and the microphone. They leveled off just above the tree tops, and then dropped, landing with their knees bent.

There was complete silence. Then people started clapping. The clapping grew louder and louder. "Way to go!" someone shouted. Several people whistled.

"They liked it," the students said, hugging each other and dancing about as groups of people surrounded them, asking questions and offering congratulations.

Lillian scanned the crowd. At least a lot of people seemed to like it. But Theodore Green and Mrs. Snell and Evie Tilson hurried across the green without even a glance in their direction.

"Again! Fly again!" Several people shouted. "Amazing!" "We never saw anything like that!" "When can we sign up for lessons?"

Harry tapped the microphone, causing it to make several explosive booming sounds. "Thanks, everyone, for coming. But Lillian won't be signing up anyone for classes until after a decision is reached by the council on Tuesday."

"We'll insist. We'll petition," a few people shouted.

As Lillian and her students pushed through the crowd, walking toward their cars, she heard snatches of conversations. "Maybe it was a trick. Maybe they just used mirrors?" "No, I think they really were...." "Aww. No one can really fly." "What about Robby...heard he...of a sudden straightened up."

Lillian looked at Charles. He was frowning. Had he heard the comments too? "How do you think the council will vote?"

Charles shook his head. "No idea. Obviously, a lot of people are for it. However, I have a suggestion for tonight. "Dinner? If you don't have other plans?"

Lillian smiled. "I don't, and I'd love to have dinner with you."

Chapter 27
Karen Gets Upset

Lillian drove home with thoughts about her upcoming dinner date with Charles tumbling in her head. How long since she'd last gone out on a date? Would it be awkward? Where might they go? A couple of new restaurants had opened. Maybe she'd suggest they try out one of those. Unless he already had a place in mind. As she unlocked the door to her apartment, her cell phone rang. It was Karen.

"Mother, I don't know what to do! Everyone's been calling me. Someone even called from the paper. What'll I tell our clients? Mr. Bryant's already been watching me with this funny look on his face. Yesterday, he had a long conference in his office with my supervisor. I'm scared he thinks he made a mistake hiring me."

Lillian gripped her phone. "Karen, for once, please listen—"

"No! And I hope the council votes against you. You're ruining my life." The phone went silent.

Lillian slowly held down her phone. An empty place spread inside her stomach. Even if Bryant Securities sounded stuffy, Karen wanted that job. But even for this much-loved and only child, Lillian would never give up flying. It would be like giving up breathing.

She walked into her bathroom and turned on the water in the tub. She squirted bubble bath oil at the gushing water and watched bubbles foam up, spread across the surface of the water and rise up the sides of the tub. She squirted another stream of bath oil at the flowing water and a third. Pushing thoughts of Karen to the back of her mind, she pictured herself soaring upward into the sky.

Chapter 28
Robby Phones Lillian

At 4:00 on Tuesday, the day of the council meeting, Robby phoned Lillian. "Can I come over?" His voice sounded urgent.

"Sure," Lillian said. "What's going on?"

"It's Dad. I need to talk to you."

After putting down the phone, Lillian walked into the kitchen, turned on the oven and took out a roll of cookie dough from the freezer compartment of her refrigerator. She sliced the cookies onto a cookie sheet and slid it into the oven.

The oven timer rang at the exact moment the door buzzer sounded. Lillian pulled the cookie sheet out of the oven, placed it on top of the stove burners and walked to the door.

"Smells good," Robby said as he walked inside. Unzipping his parka, he followed Lillian back to the kitchen. "It's nice here."

"Thanks," Lillian said. "I baked us some cookies. I thought milk and a few cookies might be in order."

"Yeah, but I need more than cookies." Robby pulled a chair back from the kitchen table and sat down. "Last night I made a decision. I decided what I want to do the rest of my life. Teach flying."

Lillian set a plate of cookies and a glass of milk in front of him. She sat in a chair opposite him. "That's a wonderful thing to want to do. But you know, of course, that as of now we don't even know if I will be able to keep on teaching it. If flying will even be allowed in town." She glanced at the clock above the door. Only a little more than three hours until the meeting was scheduled to begin.

Robby broke a cookie in half, then broke the pieces in half again. "That's the only thing I want to do. If they don't pass it, it'll ruin my whole life."

Lillian nodded. "I'd hate it too."

Robby gulped his glass of milk to the bottom. He wiped his mouth with the back of his hand. His eyes flashed. "Dad doesn't take flying seriously? He says it's great recreation, and he's glad I'm doing that instead of hanging out with my old friends. He likes you and the others in our class, but he doesn't think it would be a good career. He said it's too different, too uncertain. He thinks I should be a lawyer—like him."

Lillian pressed her fingertips together in her lap.

"I mean, my dad thinks you're great, and he hopes we get to keep flying and you get to keep teaching, but...."

Lillian stared at Robby. Could he possibly have misunderstood? Hadn't Charles just told her that he might want to learn to fly too? She softened her voice. "I'm sure your father wants what is best for you."

"But he doesn't know what's best for me. He just thinks he does." Robby stuffed a whole cookie in his mouth and stared across the room.

Lillian looked at her hands now resting on the table. A small piece of cookie dough was stuck on the cuff of her sweater sleeve. She pulled off the dough and placed it on her napkin. Robby seemed convinced of his dad's view. But regardless, he still needed his dad. She wanted to support Charles as much as possible.

"Anyway," Robby said, looking back at her. "I've already decided. That's what I'm going to do. No matter what you or anyone says."

Lillian's cell phone rang. She glanced at it, nodded at Robby and hurried back to her bedroom before answering.

"Hello, dear," Mrs. Wilson said. "I just wanted to say we'll pick you up around 7:15."

"Thanks, and could you take Robby too? He's here now and I'm planning to invite him to stay for dinner."

"We'll be glad to. Oh, I talked to Marty, and they're bringing Sally, even though it's a school night. We're all going to sit together. Marty said they'll go early to save seats. She said she's heard that a lot of people are coming."

159

When Lillian returned to the kitchen, Robby was standing in front of the refrigerator. He was looking at Sally's flying school picture that was taped to the side of the refrigerator. The muscles across his jaw were tight.

"Would you like to stay for dinner?" Lillian asked. "But I'm warning you. It's nothing fancy. Mainly leftovers."

"Sure. Thanks." He turned to face her. "You're nice, Lillian. I'm glad my dad likes you."

Lillian nodded. "Thank you. Your dad's a very nice man."

"If he approved of me teaching flying, I'd think he was a lot nicer."

Lillian thought back to her conversation with Charles at dinner the evening of the flying demonstration. He'd been understanding about her job frustrations. Sympathetic of her parenting issues. Even if Robby was right about his dad not being very interested in flying, it didn't mean he was a monster. Still, it was something to consider.

"Maybe," she said, "your dad just needs more time to get used to thinking about it. And he's right about its future being uncertain. Anyway, for now, go call him about staying for dinner before it gets too late."

Chapter 29

The Town Council Meeting

By the time Lillian, Robby and the Wilsons walked into the meeting room of the town hall, most of the seats were already taken. People were talking and laughing as they slipped off jackets and scarves and draped them over the backs of their seats. The sounds of their voices mingled in a rising hum of excitement.

At the front of the room, the mayor sat at one end of a long wooden table. He was leaning over the table talking to Don Harris, a short plump man, seated at the opposite end.

The mayor ran his fingers through his short, graying brown hair and adjusted his horn-rimmed glasses. Al Perkins, a tall, heavy-set man, sat beside the mayor, then, skipping an empty chair, was Theodore Green.

People streamed through the doors. Robby pointed across the room. "Come on, everyone. There's Dad and the Joneses."

As Lillian, Robby and the Wilsons eased past the knees of people already sitting in the row with Charles and the Joneses, Charles gathered up jackets and scarves from the seats beside them.

After they had settled into their seats, Mrs. Wilson leaned across Robby and spoke to Lillian. "Look. There's Evie Tilson and her husband."

Charles nodded "And the man and woman next to her are the Snells, our next door neighbors."

Lillian ran the tip of her tongue across her lower lip. She recognized the Snells from the demonstration on Saturday. They had been in the same group with Theodore Green. She forced a smile when they looked her way.

Mr. Wilson reached behind Mrs. Wilson and Robby and tapped Lillian's shoulder. "Here come two more council members."

Ann MacDonald, a trim, middle-aged woman with dark, curly hair, and Jack Sims, a tall, thin man, walked to the table in the front of the room. Ann MacDonald sat between Theodore Green and Al Perkins. Jack Sims sat on the other side of Theodore Green. After nodding at the other council members, Jack Sims pulled a notebook out of his briefcase and opened it. The other council members continued talking among themselves.

"Sims looks tense," Charles whispered.

Lillian nodded and clasped her hands together in her lap. Jack Sims was a thoughtful man, cautious. She'd always respected what he had to say, even if she didn't always agree with him. How would he feel about flying?

The mayor rapped his gavel on the table. "Will the meeting please, come to order?" He looked at everyone and waited until the room quieted. "The issue before us tonight is—whether to permit flying and flying lessons in Green Valley. Is there any discussion?"

A man sitting in front of Lillian stood and waved his arm. "It's terrific. I think we should have it. I—"

From across the room, Evie Tilson jumped up and glared at him. "I disagree. It would destroy our community. It would—"

The mayor rapped his gavel. "Mrs. Tilson, could we speak one at a time please?"

The man who'd been interrupted looked embarrassed and sat down. "It's all right. I said about everything I was going to say."

Evie looked around at the audience. Her chin lifted slightly. "Well. Well, I'm here to say that flying would be the worst thing ever to—"

Mr. Tilson grabbed Evie's elbow and pulled. His face was red.

"Turn loose," Evie said, yanking her arm free. "I have a right to speak."

Several people snickered, and the mayor rapped his gavel.

Evie glared at the mayor, then at her husband. She opened her mouth and closed it. She opened her mouth a second time, but again not a sound came out. Still glaring, she sat back down.

"Is there any more discussion?" the mayor asked. He looked around the room.

Ann MacDonald nodded, making her black curly hair stand out from her head. "I couldn't find any law or ordinance against it."

Theodore Green slammed the palm of his hand on the table. "Mrs. MacDonald, that's precisely because no one ever did anything like that before. How can there be a law against something that's never even been heard of?"

Several people behind Lillian shuffled their feet and whispered, "Yeah. Yeah. He's right."

Ann MacDonald put both hands on the edge of the table and rose several inches off her chair. Her cheeks turned red. "Well I—"

Theodore Green shook his head. "Just what effect do you think this would have on the young people in this town if such a thing were permitted?"

The mayor rapped the table. "Mr. Green, please allow Mrs. MacDonald to finish."

Theodore Green ignored him. "People flying? Everyone's doing fine the way they are—walking, even running—but flying? It's ridiculous! Outrageous!"

The mayor rapped again. "Mr. Green, please. Mrs. MacDonald was speaking."

Ann MacDonald nodded at the mayor. "Thank you. I thought flying looked wonderful. I want to learn how, too."

A number of people clapped, and Lillian and her students squeezed each other's hands.

Al Perkins pulled off his glasses and wiped them with a white handkerchief. He blinked at Ann MacDonald. "But we know virtually nothing about flying."

Don Harris, sitting opposite the mayor, shifted about on his chair. He glanced around the packed meeting hall. "Well, it seems kind of harmless to me. Of course, I agree absolutely that the whole idea is unbelievable. I still wonder if I really saw what I thought I saw." He glanced around the room again. "And I can project some problems that might possibly arise out of it."

Lillian shook her head. This was Don Harris's first term. Obviously, he didn't want to risk offending any possible voters regardless of their position.

Jack Sims frowned and riffled the edges of his notebook.

Evie Tilson stood up again and this time was able to find the words to speak out against flying. Also, this time Mr. Tilson didn't try to stop her. She was followed by Mrs. Snell, who echoed Evie's disapproval, then by several people who spoke in favor of flying.

Finally, the mayor rapped the table several times. "I think we've discussed this enough. Now I'm going to ask for the council members' vote. I'll call on you in alphabetical order. Mr. Green."

Theodore Green leaned forward, his eyebrows drawn together above his nose. "No. I vote no. Absolutely not in our town."

From across the room, Evie Tilson smiled at Mrs. Snell. They looked at Lillian and her students and smirked.

Lillian clinched her fingers tightly. She ran the tip of her tongue over her dry lips.

"Mr. Harris?" the mayor said.

Don Harris looked around the audience. He tugged the neck of his shirt. "Uh, yes. At least for now I'm going to vote 'yes.'"

A large number of people clapped, and Lillian crossed her arms in front of her chest and hugged herself.

"Mrs. MacDonald?" the mayor asked.

Ann McDonald straightened her shoulders as she looked at the mayor. "Yes." Her voice rang out, and the same people who'd clapped before clapped again.

"We're ahead," Robby whispered. "Two to one."

"I know," Lillian whispered.

The mayor turned sideways. "Mr. Perkins?"

Al Perkins blinked and shoved up his glasses. "I don't think we know enough about it at this time. I'll have to vote 'no.'"

Two for and two against. Lillian slid forward on her seat, her stomach as tight and prickly as if it were full of porcupine quills.

"Mr. Sims?" the mayor asked.

Jack Sims glanced down at his notebook, his hair falling across his forehead.

The room went silent. Somewhere outside a car door slammed and an engine started. A dog barked. Lillian squeezed her hands together so hard her fingernails pinched into her skin.

Jack Sims looked at the mayor then at all the people in the room facing him. "I've thought a lot about this. I've read a number of writings about flight. Also, I've discussed flying with several authorities in the areas of philosophy, religion and science."

He lifted the notebook. "I've written a summary of the major arguments considered along with my own thoughts which I'll post on the town website." He looked at the mayor and other council members. "I've come to the conclusion...." He paused and looked at his audience. "...that we should give flying a chance. I vote—'yes.'"

Robby leaped out of his chair. "We won! We won!" The people sitting both in front of him and behind him clapped and cheered.

Tears ran down Lillian's cheeks. She and her students hugged each other. The people who had been sitting behind Lillian patted her on the back. "Way to go!" "Congratulations!"

But across the room, Mr. and Mrs. Tilson and Mr. and Mrs. Snell gathered up their coats and headed for the door. Evie glared over her shoulder at Lillian then hurried after the others.

Lillian breathed in a long, deep breath. "I don't have to stop teaching. We don't have to stop flying. I can't believe it. I simply can't believe it's true."

"Let's go somewhere and celebrate," Mr. Wilson said, pulling on his coat.

"Come to my place," Lillian said. "I've already got pizzas in the freezer."

Charles grinned. "Sounds good to me. I'll pick up sodas and ice on the way." He looked at Robby. "How about you coming with me?"

"Then we're all set," Mr. Wilson said. "And we'll meet back at Lillian's."

Chapter 30

Pizza at Lillian's Apartment

Back at her apartment, Lillian turned on extra lights in the living room and placed a CD in the player. She directed the Wilsons and Joneses back to her bedroom to put their coats and gloves on her bed.

She headed into the kitchen followed by Marty, Sally and Mrs. Wilson.

"Can I help?" Mrs. Wilson and Marty asked at the same time.

"Thanks." Lillian pulled out two cookie sheets. "You can get the pizzas out of the freezer and put them on these. And take out some napkins. They're on the counter by the fridge."

The door buzzer sounded. A moment later, Robby walked into the kitchen carrying a large plastic bag of ice. "Dad's bringing in the drinks. What do I do with this?"

"Set it in the sink," Lillian said, "And then would you get some glasses out of the cupboard, please? You're taller than I."

"They passed flying," Robby said, setting eight glasses on the counter. "Now for sure I'll get to teach it!"

Frowning, Charles walked in behind Robby and set the sodas on the counter. "Changing the subject slightly, did you see the Snells' and Tilsons' faces when they were leaving? They looked ready for a fight."

"No," Mrs. Wilson said, sliding a pizza in the oven. "I didn't see their faces, but I can imagine."

"Who cares?" Mr. Wilson said, stepping beside her. "I can fly! That's what matters most to me!"

"Me too," said Sally. "I love to fly. It makes me feel like a big red balloon all full of happiness." She looked at her father who was standing in the doorway. "It makes me want to hug everyone in the whole world. And all the clouds and flowers and animals. I just want to say 'I love you' to them!"

"That would be kind of hard to do," said Harry, smiling. Stooping beside Sally, he hugged her shoulders.

Sally sighed. "I know. I just have to draw pictures of them instead."

Later, while everyone sat around the living room talking and eating, Lillian leaned forward in her easy chair. "Thank you, everyone, for your support. I never would've made it without you."

Mrs. Wilson shook her head. "We're the ones who should be thanking you."

"Absolutely!" said Mr. Wilson, swallowing a mouthful of pizza. "There hasn't been this much excitement in town for years! I've got a whole new lease on life! Remember how I said I was thinking about signing up for a photography course at the community college? Well I did. Also, Grace and I've been talking about doing some tutoring at the neighborhood center."

Grace put her hand on George's arm. "I almost forgot. I was going to tell everyone about my book. Can I do that now before it gets too late?"

The others smiled. "Yes." "Sure." "Please do."

Lillian nodded. "I remember. You said at your dinner party you wanted to wait until after the council meeting."

Mrs. Wilson nodded. "No matter how they voted, I would still have kept on writing. But if they hadn't voted 'yes,' I might have waited before I said anything about it." She took a breath.

"It's a little hard to explain, but once I learned to fly, I began seeing life differently. Flying changed how things appeared. Boundaries dissolved, and I knew deep down that the same energy force that enables me and the rest of our group to fly also flows through every other person and thing and always has and always will."

"In this remarkably basic way, every person and thing is the same. It's a bond linking everyone and

171

everything together forever—even beyond our world and universe to infinity."

"Events which once seemed coincidental or almost supernatural now appear inevitable. Such as opportunities arising when least expected and finding answers in unimagined ways and places. Flying is so wonderful that I wanted to share some of my experiences with others by writing this book."

"Can I be in your book?" Sally asked.

"Of course, but I may change your name," Mrs. Wilson said.

Marty nodded. "I'm glad you're writing about this. I totally agree with you and Sally. Such a short time ago I was so bored just doing the books for our landscaping business, and now...."

Harry stiffened. "And now what?"

"Do you know what I want to do?" Marty asked.

"What?"

"I still want to help with our business. But I loved organizing the flying demonstration. Being with all the people." She looked at Lillian. "I just know flying is going to catch on. Can I be your assistant and do some PR part time? I know I'd be good at it."

Lillian smiled. "Of course. I'd love to have your help."

Charles set his empty plate on the coffee table in front of him. "Friends, I don't know what to say. I'm glad flying can continue. It's definitely been a good experience for Robby. But what I'm hearing now sounds a little—um—out of touch with reality."

Harry sat forward. "Well I've seen enough to convince me. Charles, maybe you should do like me and sign up for Lillian's next class? Give it a try?"

Robby sat forward. "Yeah, Dad. You might see things differently. Like Mrs. Wilson said."

Marty looked at Lillian. "By the way, when do you have to go back to work?"

Lillian glanced at Sally who was sitting on the sofa beside Marty, yawning. "Actually, I plan to go by the office in the morning to discuss that."

Marty touched Harry's arm. "We probably should go. It's getting late and Sally has school in the morning."

The others nodded and began standing.

Charles cleared his throat. "Harry, would you mind dropping Robby off at our house on your way? He's got homework, and I want to stay and help Lillian clean up."

"I could help too," Robby said. "I've already done all my home...oh, I just remembered." He grinned at his father. "I do have something else I should read."

Warmth spread across Lillian's throat and cheeks.

Chapter 31

Lillian and Charles Talk

Lillian stood at the kitchen sink stacking plates. Charles set several glasses on the counter at her side. "I hope you don't mind me staying."

"Not at all. It's good of you to offer to help. Thanks."

Charles added another plate to those already in the sink. "I enjoyed our dinner the other night. You're easy to talk to."

"Thanks. So are you." Lillian turned on the water. Holding her breath, she watched the water rise slowly over the dishes.

Charles placed his left hand on the edge of the sink. His fingers were long and squared at the tips, tan except for a lighter band of skin around his ring finger. Had he been wearing a wedding ring that first time they met? She couldn't remember.

"With some differences, we've both been there," he said. "It's a bond. I've got a concern though."

"Wait." Lillian turned off the water. "Let's go in the living room."

She wiped off the counter with her dish sponge, propped it against the base of the faucet and switched off the light over the sink. She walked out of the kitchen into the living room followed by Charles.

Kicking off her clogs, she sat in her easy chair and tucked her legs up beside her.

Charles sat on the sofa at the end nearest her. He leaned towards her. "The other day I ran into one of Robby's teachers. She said he's almost a completely changed student. She said his work is superior now. On time and well done." He frowned. "But now Robby's started saying that when he finishes school, he's going to teach flying as a career."

Lillian nodded. So this was why he wanted to stay and help.

"He'd make an excellent lawyer," Charles said. "I keep telling him so. He won't even listen to me. We end up arguing."

Lillian tucked her skirt in around her feet. She forced her voice to stay even. "Robby's your son, and I'm certainly not going to tell you what to do—"

"But you do have an opinion."

"I do. Yes."

"And?"

"I think it would be helpful if you really listened to him and tried to understand."

Charles's eyes opened wide. "Wait. Let me explain. I—well, one day, I'd hoped to make him a partner in my law firm."

"And now you're afraid that that might not happen."

"Right."

Lillian shrugged. "He's only sixteen. He could change his mind several times by the time he finishes school, or he could try teaching flying and discover it isn't right for him."

"I'd hate to see him flounder about and get off course, maybe even mess up his life."

"I know. But if the only reason he became a lawyer was to please you, how happy do you think he'd be?"

Charles looked across the room. His jaw muscles tightened, but he remained silent.

Lillian watched his chest rise and fall as he breathed. Did he have any idea how much alike he and Robby were? Willful, intelligent, obstinate?

After several moments, Charles looked back at her. He smiled. "Enough about Robby for now. I'd rather talk about us—what we're going to do next. What about giving me some private flying lessons?"

"Private lessons?" Lillian sat up straight, scooting her feet off the seat of the chair onto the floor. "You're serious? From the way you've been talking, I didn't expect you to be that interested."

"I am interested. Just maybe not to the same degree as the others in your class."

Lillian smoothed her skirt over her knees. She stared at him a moment and looked away. What was really going on with him? Did he even know? Were lessons merely an excuse to spend time with her? Might his interest deepen once he'd flown? How might she feel about him if he came to value flying as much as she did?

She looked back at him and shook her head slowly. "This is all so new. I'm not ready to give private lessons. I'd rather you signed up for one of my classes."

Charles nodded. "I'm sorry. I didn't mean to rush you."

"No harm done." Lillian smiled. "But there is something I'd like to do now."

"What?"

"Dance. I haven't danced in ages. If I put in another CD, would you dance with me?"

"You bet I would." Charles stood, stretching his hand toward her.

Chapter 32
Lillian Returns to Her Office

Lillian stood in the shower with water splashing over her head and down her back as she rinsed shampoo lather from her hair. She'd waked up an hour early with her stomach feeling as if it were full of moths beating their tiny, frantic wings. If only she could know for sure if what she was about to do was the right thing.

After toweling off and combing out her damp hair, she pulled on her best wool skirt and sweater, ate a bowl of oatmeal and hurried outside to her car.

At ten minutes after eight, she stepped into the reception room of the family counseling offices. She flipped on the lights. The doors to all the offices were closed. Everything looked familiar and homey. When she walked inside her own office, she noticed that someone must have been watering the plant that sat on her bookshelf because the plant's leaves were a deep glossy green.

"Lillian! You're back!" boomed a voice from behind her.

She jumped and turned.

Will Hawkins stood in the doorway, his overcoat still buttoned. He grinned. "Didn't mean to startle you. At least this time you weren't standing on your desk." He smiled again. "I'm glad you're back. Now after seeing the demonstration, I think I understand why...."

Lillian shook her head. "Can I talk to you? Now?"

Her supervisor frowned, his eyebrows drawing together over his nose. "Certainly. But let's go back to my office."

Lillian sat on the chair in front of his desk. She took a long, deep breath. She felt the same way she had the time she sat on her first bicycle at the top of the driveway and prepared to lift both feet off the ground.

Will Hawkins shut the door and sat at his desk. He tugged the knot on his tie. "What's going on?"

Lillian pressed her fingertips together in her lap. "I've been thinking a lot about things." She glanced out the window. The early morning sun cast red-gold streaks across the sky. Even this early, people were hurrying along the sidewalks. The traffic light at the corner turned from red to green. She swallowed. "I want to resign my job. I want to teach flying full time."

Will Hawkins swiveled his chair to the side. He rested his elbows on the arms of his chair and laced his fingers together in front of his chest. He stared out the window. Slowly he turned to face her. "I guess I'm not surprised. Disappointed, but not surprised. When I saw the demonstration on Saturday, it occurred to me that, at some point, you might want to do something like this."

Lillian hesitated. "I thought about just asking for a leave of absence. But I knew if things worked out, I wouldn't be coming back."

He nodded. "I understand. You're a good counselor, Lillian, and I hate giving you up. But I won't try to stop you. And I wish you luck. Now when did you want this to go into effect?"

Lillian smoothed a pleat in her skirt. She swallowed. "What I'd like to do is come back on Monday and work a month. That will give me time to talk to all my clients and get my records in order."

Chapter 33

Lillian Makes Telephone Calls

As soon as Lillian returned home she called Karen on her cell phone. Karen didn't pick up and her call went to voice mail. Lillian touched "end" and called the Bryant Securities' office. She asked to speak to Karen. The receptionist put her on hold. Lillian sketched little boxes on a scrap of paper. She'd encouraged her clients to speak out and to stand up for themselves. It was past time for her to do the same with her own daughter.

The receptionist came back on. "Mam, I'm sorry but Miss Brown is in a conference with Mr. Bryant and can't be disturbed."

"A conference? Oh, my."

"Yes, mam. Would you like to leave a message?"

"Yes. This is her mother. Would you please ask her to call me?"

Lillian was sorry for whatever Karen's problems were. But in spite of them, starting now, she was going to treat her the way she would any other adult who was fully capable of taking care of herself. And that included insisting that Karen treat her with respect and listen to her side of things for a change.

After flying around her apartment once to relax, Lillian called Sylvia. Sylvia answered on the third ring. In the background came the sounds of children's voices and a tinny recording of "Old McDonald's Farm."

"I really need to talk to you," Lillian said as soon as Sylvia said "hello." "You're my oldest friend. I've neglected you terribly and I want to apologize."

There was a long pause. "Lillian," Sylvia said, "I don't know what to say. I watched you at the flying demonstration. I had no idea it would be so...so...."

"Then you're not angry? Everything's all right?"

Sylvia laughed. "Well, I've been thinking about the other day when we met for lunch? It suddenly came to me that you'd simply gotten bored with Ed and me. You wanted to dump us but didn't know how. Then when I saw you fly, I realized how far apart we'd grown. Ed and I talked about it. We never dreamed you could ever do something like that."

"That doesn't matter. We can still be friends. But we do need to talk. Look, could you and Ed come for dinner Friday night? Seven o'clock? Things are a lot more settled in my life now. And I promise, this time nothing will get in the way."

"And if you and Ed want to, we could sing around the piano after dinner. I always enjoyed that. And I've been so busy, I haven't touched my piano in weeks."

Sylvia hesitated. "I'll have to check with Ed. Listen I've got to go. It's snack time for the kids."

Lillian slowly held down her phone. At least Sylvia hadn't said, "No," or yelled, "Get lost!" She wouldn't have blamed her if she had. But was Sylvia right? Had they already grown too far apart?

Chapter 34
Karen Drops By

Midafternoon, the door buzzer sounded. Lillian looked through the peep hole in her front door. Karen stood on the porch jamming her keys in the side compartment of her shoulder bag. Lillian held her breath as she opened the door.

Karen rushed inside. "Mom, I got your message. But I can't stay long. Bryant's is having a fancy dinner for some clients tonight, and I have to go to that." She pulled off her scarf. Long strands of her auburn hair fell across her shoulders.

"At least take off your coat and sit down," Lillian said. "And how about some hot chocolate?"

Karen shook her head and remained standing. "I can't stay that long. But first I have to tell you something. Mr. Bryant called me in his office this morning and—"

"Wait!" Lillian raised her hand, palm toward Karen, with her fingers splayed out like a police officer, saying, "Stop!" She looked Karen straight in her eyes. "First *I* want to tell *you* something. I'm sorry if Mr. Bryant is upset with you, but —"

"Mom, wait —"

"No. You wait. I'm through assuming responsibility for everything that goes wrong and—"

"Mom, stop it." Karen grabbed Lillian's shoulders and shook her. "You've got it wrong. You're wonderful!"

Lillian's mouth dropped open.

"Mr. Bryant called me in his office today. He wanted to know why I wasn't up there flying with you." Karen looked into Lillian's eyes. "He said he and Mrs. Bryant went to both the demonstration and the town meeting. He said he thinks I have a good future with the company, but being a stock broker is stressful. He said he thought I should learn to relax more, and why didn't I take up flying like he and Mrs. Bryant are going to do."

Karen threw her arms around Lillian. "Mom, on Saturday can I come watch you fly?"

Lillian's eyes filled with tears. Her throat tightened. She tightened her arms around Karen, holding her close. "Next to flying, I can't think of anything I'd like more!"

Karen pulled away and looked at her watch. "I've got to run," Halfway out the door she turned back around. "I almost forgot. Dad came by after the demonstration. He said he might not want to get married again anytime soon. He said first he wanted to learn how to fly."

Lillian gasped. "No kidding? Oh my goodness!"

After Karen left Lillian plumped the sofa pillows and straightened the magazines on the coffee table. What about Karen wanting to come watch on Saturday? And her ex wanting to learn to fly? She twirled around the living room to waltz music coming from her radio. And on top of that, Sylvia and Ed were coming to dinner tomorrow. At least, since Sylvia hadn't called back to say otherwise, she assumed they were coming.

And miracle of miracles. She could keep on teaching and flying—full time!

Unbelievable! Straightening up her apartment could wait. Everything could. She didn't want to waste another moment.

Dashing back to her bedroom, she changed into jeans and a heavy sweater. Next, she pulled on her red and white knit cap, jamming it down over her ears, and knotted her scarf around her neck. She rushed outside, still working her fingers into her knit gloves, jumped in her car and drove along the interstate heading toward the meadow.

Chapter 35
The Meadow

When Lillian stepped out of her car the air was still. It was mild for a late winter afternoon. Soon it would be spring. Very soon. In fact it might already be spring.

"HOOORAY," she shouted, cupping her hands on either side of her mouth as she looked up at the sky. "HOOORAY!" She dashed into the middle of the meadow, stopped and stretched her arms over her head. Then lowering her arms and stooping to the ground, she jumped. The balls of her feet pushed against the earth, unleashing all the pent up energy of a coiled and compressed spring suddenly released.

Air whooshed past her as she zoomed toward the sky, the ends of her scarf flapping at her sides like tiny red and white striped flags. Oh, the joy of it all. The joy of it. Life was so wonderful she simply had to fly.

High above the ground, she leaned forward, leveling her body. Then she flew faster than she'd ever flown before. She angled her body up and flew still higher. She flew into a cloud so enormous it was like flying up through thousands of feet of white icy mist. The moisture dampened her cheeks and chin and the strands of reddish hair poking out of her knit cap. Her body tingled with the cold air rushing past her.

Finally, emerging from the top of the cloud, she flew into air current after air current after air current. The currents carried her in wide, sweeping spirals high above the meadow which, when she glanced down, was only a small patch of golden brown circled by trees still bare from winter.

Rolling onto her stomach, she stretched out her arms from her body and relaxed her fingers. She loosened the muscles in her entire body. Breathing slowly and evenly, she let the currents continue to carry her as if she were merely a feather or a leaf.

Far below her, a flock of geese flew past. Their honking calls wafted upward and she smiled. Such wonderful creatures. So amazing. In the far distance, the skyline of Green Valley slid into view, only a rim of tiny silhouetted buildings. Beautiful. Such a very special town.

Still smiling, she wiggled her toes inside her wool socks and sneakers. *Here everything is possible. Everything.* The words were a song inside her.

The End

Acknowledgments

First and foremost thank you, Ann Campanella, editor and publisher of The Bridge, poet, author and years-long dear friend. Without your excitement about this book along with your knowledge and expertise of the publishing world and many words of encouragement, *Lillian's Flying School* might never have taken flight.

Also, thank you, writer friends: Jean Beatty, Ann Campanella, Allison Elrod, Anne Holden, Lisa Williams Kline, Barbara Mayer, Carolyn Noell and Judy Stacy who over too many years to count have given, so freely and honestly, your support alongside your critiques.

Thank you, Adrienne and Ken Pedersen, close friends, for your interest and many words of encouragement. Thank you, Ken, for reading the manuscript and for your technical assistance in preparing the photo of the cover art.

Thank you, Laurie Walker, Mindfulness instructor, Founder and Blogger@ Namaste Connections, for your beautiful, inspiring words on the back cover.

Thank you, Judy Freeman, for sharing your photography talent by taking the author photo.

About the Author

Nancy Lammers holds a B.A. degree from Agnes Scott College and a Master of Human Development and Learning degree from UNC-Charlotte. She is a former counselor in a nonprofit children's services organization. She also worked as a temporary public school teacher in Charlotte, North Carolina, and as a research assistant in the biology department at Emory University.

She is the author of *Surf Riding,* a collection of short stories, published by Main Street Rag Publishing Company. Her short stories, poems and children's stories have been published in journals and magazines.

Nancy is retired and lives in Davidson, North Carolina. In addition to writing, she enjoys watercolor painting and playing her violin, mandolin and bowed psaltery in various ensembles and community organizations.

THE BRIDGE

A medium that transports
story from inspiration to creation.
Our desire is that authors and readers
will be affirmed through
creativity and the written word.

More books from The Bridge

www.TheBridgeBooks.com

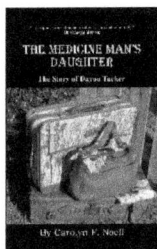

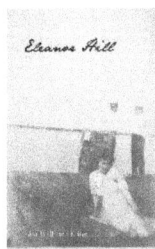

Motherhood: Lost and Found, an award-winning memoir, takes the reader on a journey where horses, Alzheimer's disease and infertility intersect, connecting the reader to the heartbeat and resilience of the human spirit. Available in softcover, Kindle and audiobook.

The Medicine Man's Daughter is an inspiring, coming-of-age account of a Liberian refugee who escapes civil war by traveling to Charlotte. Embraced by her church community, Dayou Tucker, the daughter of a medicine man, faces cultural challenges as well as hepatitis. Available in softcover.

Eleanor Hill, a historical novel and winner of the North Carolina Juvenile Literature Award, is the sweeping saga of a young woman who longs for adventures outside Atlantic Grove, her isolated North Carolina fishing village. Available in softcover and Kindle.

www.TheBridgeBooks.com